P9-DCY-723

3 5 7 9 10 8 6 4

Published in 2009 by Ebury Press, an imprint of Ebury Publishing

A Random House Group Company

Text copyright © Miss Hope 2009
Photography © Ebury Press 2009

Miss Hope has asserted her right to be identified as the author of this
Work in accordance with the Copyright, Designs and Patents Act 1988

The Random House Group Limited Reg. No. 954009

Addresses for companies within the Random House Group can be found
at **www.randomhouse.co.uk**

A CIP catalogue record for this book is available from the British Library

The Random House Group Limited supports The Forest Stewardship
Council (FSC), the leading international forest certification organisation.
All our titles that are printed on Greenpeace approved FSC certified
paper carry the FSC logo. Our paper procurement policy can be found
at **www.rbooks.co.uk/environment**

To buy books by your favourite authors and register for offers visit
www.rbooks.co.uk

Printed and bound by Firmengruppe APPL, aprinta druck, Wemding, Germany

ISBN 9780091932664

Every effort has been made to contact copyright holders. Please contact
the publishers with any queries.

Please note that conversions to imperial weights and measures are
suitable equivalents and not exact.

Design: Smith & Gilmour
Photography: Cristian Barnett and Dan Jones

For
Mr Greenwood,
my wise owl.

CONTENTS

HELLO CHUMS!

Miss Hope here, your favourite British confectioner.

In the following pages of my jolly sweet scrapbook you will discover a plethora of delicious recipes – some very traditional, others a tad quirky. Rather like me, in fact. Be warned, however, I will not put up with any nonsense; I expect you to pay attention and have a clean hankie and a sharp pencil to hand at all times.

You can probably guess that I come from a family of teachers. I grew up surprisingly quietly in Sunderland, in the very friendly north-east of England. Picture me, eight years old, clattering off to school in my Start-rite Classics, enormous navy knickers and dragging a satchel stuffed with Pink Panther bars and *Twinkle* magazines.

In the long, l-o-n-g summer holidays, my sister Maggy and I played sweet shops in our back garden. There were leaves and seed pods for sweets and pebbles for money. Tiny Tears popped by for some sherbet lemons, Sindy always chose the strawberry bonbons, and occasionally Panda and Holly Hobbie popped by for a quarter of wine gums on their way to the hairdresser's for a wash and set.

These were simple days when we went to bed when it was still light, played Buckaroo in our neon catsuits and Mum rinsed our hair with vinegar. We had never seen a duvet or eaten muesli, and the telly was still black and white. My dad used to whack the monumental machine with his slipper to get reception.

A grillion years and lots of duvet days and muesli breakfasts later, here we are, my favourite husband Mr Greenwood and I, with our very own sweet shops.

At Hope and Greenwood we get very excited about the best of British confectionery. Mr Greenwood and I have tramped valleys and dales for many hours to find the most splendid hand-made sweet recipes in this lovely land, and now we want to share some of our favourites with you. We really hope you like them as much as we do, but take note, dear chums, that we are sticklers for the very best ingredients money can buy. So, before you get stuck in to our recipes, arm yourself with oodles of fresh cream and butter and buy shares in vanilla pods.

If you peep into our sweet shops at night, you might be lucky enough to spot the Hope and Greenwood sugar gnomes tirelessly creating the most beautiful confections. They make absolutely sure that our shelves are always laden with extra-fizzy sherbet lemons, rhubarb and custard, apple pie chocolate, award-winning Kir Royale truffles and crumbly butter fudge.

So, welcome to our scrapbook of Hopeylicious secret recipes. Feast on coconut ice, pulled butter toffee, toffee apples, fudge, chocolates, nougats, marshmallows, syrup sponge nuggets, buttered brazils, sticky toffee truffles and sherbet lemon marshmallows. Your house will smell like home, you will buy a new apron, you will be the envy of all your neighbours – even the curtain-twitcher at number 32 will come out and pat you on the back.

Toodle pip!

Miss Hope

HOPE AND GREENWOOD
MILK AMARETTO
HANDMADE IN ENGLAND
A lovely cup of creamy, dreamy amaretto truffle topped with
an almondy biscuit. Like an almost-version of tea and biscuits

HOPE AND GREENWOOD
PETTICOAT FONDANTS
HANDMADE IN ENGLAND
The prettiest of all our confections

ARE YOU SITTING COMFORTABLY?

Before we go any further, you ought to know that I am a bit bossy. I expect you to do exactly as you are told, or you will have to stand in the corner until playtime. Isn't that right, Mr Greenwood?

1 ★ **Please do:** Pay attention. When I say 'use a deep heavy-bottomed pan' (4 litres or 5–6 pints big), which I do quite a lot, you simply must or you will end up with toffee down the front of your nightie.

2 ★ **Please do:** Refrain from eating hot toffee. It is really, really hot, it will burn you and you will cry. Don't do it, you crazy person, you.

3 ★ **Please do:** Buy a sugar thermometer. I beg you on my knees, grasping at your vestments; it doesn't cost too much and it is the tool for the job. (Please see my notes on temperatures on the opposite page and also where to buy a thermometer – stockists listed on page 126.)

4 ★ **Please do:** Watch your pots boil. Don't wander off for a bubble bath or pop into Margery's next door with a pie. Some of the recipes need you to stare at the pan while they cook. If you don't, you're in danger of setting the kitchen alight and it will require a crew of sweaty firemen to put it out.

5 ★ **Please do:** Melt chocolate with care; melt it using as little heat as possible, as this will stop it going white when it sets. Take particular care with white chocolate, which melts in no time at all and can burn very easily.

6 ★ **Please do:** Use a wooden spoon when cooking toffee. A plastic spatula will melt like the Wicked Witch of the West.

7 ★ **Please do:** Leave the Brillo pad under the sink. The best way to wash a pan covered in toffee or fudge is to fill it with water and put it back on the heat. As if by magic, the toffee will just bubble off.

8 ★ **Please do:** Make sweets for your neighbours and friends. They will be green with envy for your blissful domestic lifestyle.

SOME DULL BUT IMPORTANT RULES ABOUT TEMPERATURES

Sugar is a fickle thing, one minute it's all 'Coo-wee, look at me, lovely golden bubbling sugar in a pan', and the next thing you are flapping at the smoke alarm with the nearest thing to hand – possibly a tea towel or a small child.

If you have ignored my advice above and not bought a sugar thermometer (tut-tut and shame on you), you can use the following techniques to make my recipes without one.

Soft Ball 113–118°C (235–245°F) is used for fudges and fondants.

Drop a little of the syrup into a glass of cold water. Leave it for a couple of minutes then roll it between your fingers, it should form a soft ball.

Hard Ball 118–130°C (245–265°F) is used for marshmallows, caramels and nougats.

Drop a little of the syrup into a glass of cold water. Leave it for a couple of minutes then roll it between your fingers, it should form a firm ball, but it should not be rock hard.

Small Crack 132–143°C (270–290°F) is used for toffees and boiled sweets.

Drop a little of the syrup into a glass of cold water. It should separate into small pieces, though they should be hard, not brittle.

Hard Crack 149–154°C (300–310°F) is used for really hard toffees.

Drop a little of the syrup into a glass of cold water. It should separate into brittle threads and the mixture should start to turn a golden colour.

STORAGE

Really there is little point telling you how to store your confections as they will be eaten faster than you can say 'magic knickers'. But, just in case you are puritanical, wise or delusional here are some thoughts about storage.

★ **Truffles** made with fresh cream should be kept in the fridge and eaten within 3-4 days. If you freeze them they will last for two months.

★ **Fudge** can be stored in the fridge for up to two weeks, please allow it to warm to room temperature before you eat it. It will also freeze well for two months.

★ **Toffee** should be kept in an airtight tin and will last for a week or so. It helps to wrap the pieces individually in parchment paper or they will stick together in a flash. English Almond Butter Toffee should be kept and served directly from the fridge.

★ **Mr Greenwood's Buttered Brazils** should be placed in an airtight tin and sent directly to Mr Greenwood.

★ **Coconut Ice** should be stored in an airtight container and will last for about a month.

★ **Mallows** should be stored in an airtight tin lined with parchment and will last for about a week. They are, however, best eaten as fresh as possible.

★ **Nougat** should be stored in a cool, dry place for up to two weeks. I find putting it in the fridge makes it ooze unpleasantly.

★ **Turkish Delight** should be stored in an airtight tin lined with parchment dusted with icing sugar and cornflour, it will last for about one month.

★ **Pastilles** should be kept in the fridge and last a fleeting two days.

★ **Miss Hope** should be stored on her sofa with a gin and tonic and a copy of *Sweet Spot Weekly*, her décolletage should be lightly dusted in icing sugar and perfumed with violet syrup. She should last another 30 years or so.

Now let's begin.

HOPE AND GREENWOOD

SPLENDID CONFECTIONERY

Chocolate

CHAPTER ONE

MIDNIGHT DARK TRUFFLES

★ **Makes 25–30 deep, dark, stylish truffles**

★ **Take 30 minutes to make; cool and set overnight.**

200ml (7fl oz)
   double cream
25g (1oz) butter
200g (7oz) good-quality
   dark chocolate, broken
   into small bits
Cocoa powder, to dust

25–30 foil sweet cases
   (optional)

Once, when strolling down the Champs Elysées, my chum Coco said to me, she said: 'Miss H, keep it simple; style is everlasting, you may want to rethink the hot pants.' So, on her sound advice, here is the simplest, most marvellously stylish truffle recipe for those among my chums who like it dark with a bitter bite.

Once you have the basic truffle mix you can start to create your own flavours; here I have started the ball rolling with stem ginger, rum and whisky.

★ Pop the cream and butter into a saucepan and heat until simmering, without letting it boil. Be careful not to let it burn or catch on the bottom of the pan.

★ Place the broken chocolate in a bowl, pour over the hot butter and cream mix and give it a brisk stir. Set aside, but check it to make sure that the chocolate has melted. Give it a stir to help it along, if need be.

★ Chill the mixture until it is firm – it will seem impossibly, scarily runny, but I promise you it will firm up admirably in time. It is best to cover the bowl with cling film and ban it to the fridge overnight. (*I am impossibly impatient, however, and I have been known to leave the mix outside in my garden on a snowy day to cool down as fast as possible!*)

P.T.O.

★ Line a flat 39 × 35cm (15¼ × 13¾in) baking sheet with a piece of baking parchment. Remove the truffle mixture from the fridge and, using a teaspoon, take a dollop of the now miraculously firm mixture. Using the palms of your hands, roll it into a ball. Be quick, as you don't want to melt the chocolate.

★ Tip some cocoa powder into a shallow bowl or plate and roll the now-truffle balls in the cocoa until they are coated all over. Place each finished truffle into a pretty foiled sweet case on the baking sheet, if you so wish.

VARIATIONS

STEM GINGER TRUFFLES

Remove 4 nuggets of stem ginger (the sort that comes in a jar), drain off the syrup and chop reasonably finely. When you remove the truffle mix from the fridge it will be cold and firm. Add the chopped ginger and proceed to shape and roll the truffles as above.

RUM TRUFFLES

Simply add 2 tablespoons of rum as you heat the cream and butter, and once you've shaped the truffles, roll them in chocolate strands or chocolate vermicelli instead of cocoa powder.

WHISKY TRUFFLES

Simply add 2 tablespoons of whisky as you heat the cream and butter.

STRAWBERRY
SHORTCAKE TRUFFLES

There is a centuries-old custom that if you break a double strawberry in half and share it with someone, they will fall in love with you. Therefore, one would have to be very careful about who you shared your Strawberry Shortcake Truffle with. I would absolutely not wish to encourage affection from Hans Rollo the Human Slinky.

★ First, make the 'jam'. Place the strawberries and the caster sugar in a heavy-bottomed pan with a splash of water. Stir and bring to the boil, then simmer for about 20 minutes until the jam is thick. It is very hot so do not be tempted to taste it. Set aside to cool until it turns paste-like.

★ Pop the cream into a saucepan and heat it until very warm, without letting it boil. Remove from the heat.

★ Place the chocolate bits in a bowl. Pour the hot cream over the chocolate and stir until the chocolate has melted. Stir in the strawberry flavouring. Leave to cool in the fridge for 20 minutes. Roughly stir in the jam, then return the bowl to the fridge until firm, preferably overnight.

★ Pop the shortbread biscuits into a food processor and whizz until they are reduced to crumbs. Tip the crumbs into a shallow bowl.

★ Line a flat 39 × 35cm (15¼ × 13¾in) baking sheet with a piece of baking parchment. Using a teaspoon, take a dollop of the strawberry truffle mixture and roll it into a ball. Carefully take each truffle ball and roll it in the shortbread crumbs, gently pressing the crumbs in as you go. Continue until all the truffles are coated in the crumb.

★ **Makes 15–20 truffles**

★ **Take about 30 minutes to make; up to 12 hours for setting.**

100ml (4fl oz) double cream
150g (5oz) milk chocolate, broken into small bits
½ tsp strawberry flavouring
75g (3oz) shortbread biscuits (bought ones are fine)

For the 'jam'
250g (9oz) strawberries, hulled
100g (4oz) caster sugar

Handy Hint
If you want to cheat, use 2 tablespoons of good strawberry jam instead of making your own.

CHOCOLATE LIFE IS SWEET

PEPPERMINT CRACKERS

During the Middle Ages the smiley folk of Great Britain used crushed peppermint to whiten their teeth; it is also known to scare off mice. This recipe combines a soothing mint cracknel running through a sliver of dark chocolate. I don't believe it will scare off mice, but I urge you to give it a go as toothpaste.

★ Grease a flat 39 × 35cm (15¼ × 13¾in) baking sheet with butter.
★ First, make the peppermint cracknel. Place the sugar and water into a heavy-bottomed pan over a low heat. Stir continuously with a wooden spoon until the sugar has dissolved – this takes about 3 minutes (see Handy Hint, below). Add the peppermint oil and stir.
★ Bring the mixture to a boil and, without stirring, boil gently for around 10 minutes until the syrup is a golden brown. Tip the mixture out onto the greased baking sheet and leave to cool.
★ Place the broken-up chocolate into a bowl with the groundnut oil and place over a pan of simmering water, taking care that the bottom of the bowl does not touch the water. Melt the chocolate slowly. Stir in the peppermint oil. Remove from the heat.
★ Pop the double cream into a pan and heat, without boiling. Pour the hot cream over the chocolate mixture and stir.
★ Using a rolling pin, crush the cooled peppermint cracknel into small shards. Add the shards to the chocolate mixture and mix well.
★ Line a 20cm (8in) square baking tin with baking parchment. Pour the mixture into the tin and cool. Once cold, turn the chocolate slab out onto a board, remove the parchment and cut into cracker-sized squares.

★ **Makes 15–20 soothing squares**

★ **Take 30 minutes to make; cool overnight.**

Butter, for greasing
400g (14oz) good-quality
  dark chocolate, broken
  into small bits
2 tsp groundnut oil
1 tsp peppermint oil
100ml (4fl oz) double cream

For the peppermint cracknel
100g (4oz) granulated
  sugar
100ml (4fl oz) water
5 drops of peppermint oil

Handy Hint
Stir the peppermint cracknel with a wooden spoon while heating to dissolve the sugar, but use the back of a metal spoon to check for any remaining sugar crystals.

ROSE AND VIOLET CREAMS

★ **Makes 20 'no-cook' easy-peasy fondant rose creams and 20 violet creams**

★ **Take 40 minutes to make; cool and set overnight.**

Rose Creams
3 tbsp double cream
Pink food colouring
3 tbsp rose syrup
275g (10oz) icing sugar
200g (7oz) milk chocolate, broken into small bits
1 tsp groundnut oil
20 crystallised rose petals, to decorate

20 sweet cases, (optional)

The sun is shining, briefly. Take my arm and let us stroll at leisure through my walled garden, plucking the occasional pink cabbage rose and letting our skirts skim the delicate petals of the shrinking violets. All too soon it will be time to put the bins out, feed the cat and microwave an Ocean Pie.

LET'S START WITH THE ROSE CREAMS

★ Place the double cream, 1 drop (yes, only 1 drop) of pink food colouring and the rose syrup into a bowl and mix well.

★ Sift the icing sugar over the cream mixture and stir to combine. This is a little like making pizza dough, so tip the mixture out onto a worksurface lightly dusted with icing sugar and knead the fondant with your hands until it all comes together in a firm ball. Place the fondant in the fridge to firm up for about 30 minutes.

★ Using your hands, roll teaspoon-sized lumps of mixture into balls then flatten them slightly and place on a plate. Continue until you have a plate full of flattened disks.

★ Heat 5cm (2in) of water in a pan. Pop a heatproof bowl on top of the pan, making sure that the bottom of the bowl is not touching the water. Place the milk chocolate and the groundnut oil in the bowl and warm until melted. Remove from the heat and cool for 10 minutes.

★ Line a flat 39 × 35cm (15¼ × 13¾in) baking sheet with a piece of baking parchment. Carefully take a fondant disk, one at a time, and, using two forks, dip it in the melted chocolate until coated all over.

LIFE IS SWEET CHOCOLATE

P.T.O.

Be quick about it, as you don't want to melt the fondant. Place the coated fondant ball onto the baking parchment. Top each chocolate with a crystallised rose petal and leave to cool and set in a cool place. Place in sweet cases to serve, if you like.

NOW FOR VIOLET CREAMS ...

Now for Violet Creams...
3 tbsp double cream
Purple food colouring
2 tbsp violet syrup
225g (8oz) icing sugar
200g (7oz) dark chocolate,
   broken into small bits
1 tsp groundnut oil
crystallised violet petals,
   to decorate

20 sweet cases, (optional)

★ Place the double cream, 1 drop (yes, only 1 drop) of purple food colouring and the violet syrup into a bowl and mix well.

★ Sift the icing sugar over the cream mixture and stir to combine. This is a little like making pizza dough, so tip the mixture out onto a worksurface lightly dusted with icing sugar and knead the fondant with your hands until it all comes together in a firm ball. Place the fondant in the fridge to firm up for about 30 minutes.

★ Take the fondant out of the fridge and, using your hands, roll teaspoon-sized lumps of mixture into balls then flatten them slightly. Continue until you have a plate full of flattened disks.

★ Heat 5cm (2in) of water in a pan. Pop a heatproof bowl on top of the pan, making sure that the bottom of the bowl is not touching the water. Place the dark chocolate and the groundnut oil in the bowl and warm until melted. Remove from the heat and cool for 10 minutes.

★ Line a flat 39 x 35cm (15¼ x 13¾in) baking sheet with a piece of baking parchment. Carefully take the fondant disks, one at a time, and, using two forks, dip in the melted chocolate until coated all over. Be quick about it, you don't want to melt the fondant. Place the coated fondant disk onto the baking parchment. Top each chocolate with a crystallised violet petal and leave to cool and set in a cool place. Place in sweet cases to serve, if you like.

LIFE IS SWEET CHOCOLATE

SYRUP SPONGE NUGGETS

Tate and Lyle's Golden Syrupy sponge served with lashings of vanilla custard is Wingnut's (our 18-year-old son) favourite pudding. So in a moment akin to George V, I decided to combine vanilla-laced chocolate with gloopy syrup sponge. I think you will like it, it is certainly an unexpected filling, if a little eccentric; a wonderful cross twixt pudding and chocolate.

★ Take the golden syrup and whack it in a pan with the butter, then melt it gently until it is all runny and oozy. Put the crumbled sponge cake into a bowl and pour the syrup mixture onto it, mixing well until all the syrup has soaked into the sponge. Okay, you can try it. There is no stopping you, is there?

★ Place 5cm (2in) of hot water in a pan and heat. Pop a heatproof bowl on top of the pan, making sure that the bottom of the bowl is not touching the water. Place the white chocolate in the bowl and very gently warm it until melted. Remove from the heat and set aside to cool, but check to make sure that the chocolate has melted.

★ Pour the hot chocolate over the syrup sponge and mix together until they are united in a golden marriage of syrup and cakiness. Place in the fridge overnight until the mixture is firm.

★ Using a teaspoon, take a dollop of the mixture and, using the palms of your hands, roll it into a nugget and drop it onto a clean plate. Continue until you have a plateful of golden nuggets, then return them to the fridge to firm up again.

★ **Makes 25–30 syrupy nuggets**

★ **Take 20 minutes to make; overnight plus 2 hours in total to cool and set.**

100g (4oz) golden syrup
25g (1oz) butter
100g (4oz) crumbled sponge cake (that's 5 shop-bought fairy cakes, as it happens)
200g (8oz) white chocolate, broken into small bits

For the vanilla chocolate coating
400g (14oz) white chocolate, broken into small bits
Seeds from 1 vanilla pod

Chocolate stars (optional)

P.T.O.

★ To make the vanilla chocolate coating, place 5cm (2in) of hot water in a pan and heat. Pop a heatproof bowl on top of the pan, making sure that the bottom of the bowl is not touching the water. Place the white chocolate and the seeds scraped from the vanilla pod into the bowl and gently warm until melted, stirring to distribute the vanilla seeds. Remove from the heat.

★ Line a flat 39 x 35cm (15¼ x 13¾in) baking sheet with a piece of baking parchment. Carefully take each golden nugget and, using two forks, dip the nugget in the melted white chocolate until coated all over. Place the coated nugget on the baking sheet. Continue until all the nuggets are coated with the chocolate then sprinkle with the chocolate stars, if using. (You will have chocolate left but you need to keep it not eat it!) Leave the nuggets to cool and pop them in the fridge to set. When set, warm the white chocolate once again and coat the nuggets for a second time. Leave to cool, serve, stand back and accept the applause.

Sweet Stuff

Golden Syrup was invented in 1883 by Scottish businessman Abram Lyle. In 1904 it was registered as a trademark and in 2007 Guinness World Records declared the mark to be Britain's oldest brand. Sweet.

BLACK FOREST TRUFFLES

★ **Makes 25–30 unctuous truffles**

★ **Take 20 minutes to make; cool and set overnight.**

250g (9oz) cherries
100g (4oz) caster sugar
200g (7oz) white chocolate, broken into small bits
2 tbsp kirsch
200g (7oz) good-quality dark chocolate, broken into small bits
2 tsp groundnut oil
Cocoa powder, to dust

25–30 sweet cases, (optional)

Repeat, indulgently, after me:
    'Chocolate, cherries, kirsch and cream.
      Chocolate, cherries, kirsch and cream.
      Chocolate, cherries, kirsch and cream.'
Stop it! Stop it! Have you no shame?

★ Stone and chop the cherries then place them in a heavy-bottomed pan with the caster sugar and a splash of water. Stir and bring to the boil, then simmer for about 20 minutes until the 'jam' is thick. Be careful that it does not burn and do not be tempted to taste it – it is very hot. Set aside in the fridge to cool; it will turn thick and pasty like a 17-year-old emerging from his bedroom after four days.

★ Place 5cm (2in) of water in a pan and heat. Pop a heatproof bowl on top of the pan, making sure that the bottom of the bowl is not touching the water. Put the white chocolate bits in the bowl and gently warm it through until melted. White chocolate melts extremely quickly, so keep an eye on it; this is not a good time to go off and clean out the hamster cage.

★ Once melted, give it a brisk stir and mix in the kirsch and the cherry jam; it will turn a delightful princess-pink colour. Return to the fridge until firm, preferably overnight.

★ Line a flat 39 × 35cm (15¼ × 13¾in) baking sheet with a piece of baking parchment. Using a teaspoon, take a dollop of the cherry truffle mixture and, using the palms of your hands, roll it into a ball and drop it onto the baking sheet. Be quick, as you don't want to melt the chocolate. Dispatch the tray of truffles to the fridge for about 30 minutes so they firm up again.

★ Place 5cm (2in) of water in a pan and heat. Pop a heatproof bowl on top of the pan, as before, and place the dark chocolate and groundnut oil in the bowl. Gently warm the chocolate through until melted. Remove from the heat.

★ Carefully take each fruity truffle ball and, using two forks, dip the ball in the melted dark chocolate until coated all over. Place the coated truffle ball back on the baking sheet. Continue until all your balls are coated with the chocolate. You see, chocolate-making can be so much fun!

★ Place in sweet cases to serve, if you like, then dust with cocoa powder.

Handy Hint

If you want to cheat, just use 2 tablespoons of black cherry conserve instead of making your own 'jam'.

GARDEN MINT 'PEAS'

★ **Makes 50–60 pea-sized truffles**

★ **Take 30 minutes to make; 3 hours to overnight to cool and set, depending on your patience.**

200ml (7fl oz) double cream
25g (1oz) butter
2 drops of peppermint oil
200g (7oz) good-quality dark chocolate, broken into small bits
60g (2½oz) garden mint leaves (that's about 3 supermarket-sized packets)
8 tbsp caster sugar

Handy Hint
Counts as one of your five-a-day (and the cheque's in the post).

When I am out for supper I tend to forego coffee for fresh mint tea – so clean and refreshing. The minty centre to this delicious pea-sized truffle is gentle and subtle, while the crunchy, garden-mint sugar coating makes the pleasure buds along the side of my mouth go all jiggy with anticipation. It is a delight after supper, both cleansing and regenerating, like a walk in the rain with David Cassidy.

★ Pop the cream and butter into a saucepan and heat, without letting it boil. When the mixture is hot, remove it from the heat and add the 2 drops of peppermint oil; no more, no less.

★ Put the broken chocolate into a bowl. Pour the cream over the chopped-up chocolate, give it a brisk stir and set it aside, but check it to make sure the chocolate has melted.

★ Cool the mixture in the fridge until it is firm; overnight is best.

★ Line a flat 39 × 35cm (15¼ × 13¾in) baking sheet with a piece of baking parchment. Using a teaspoon, take a pea-sized amount of the mixture, roll it into a ball and drop it onto the baking sheet. Repeat until all the mixture is rolled into 'peas', then set aside.

★ Place the mint leaves and caster sugar into a mortar and pestle (you may need to do this in batches) and bash it up, as if it were your ex, until the mint and sugar are combined in a fragrant emerald-green sherbet.

★ Roll the truffle peas in the mint sugar until they are coated all over, pressing the minty sugar into the 'peas' as you go. Place on the baking sheet and leave in a cool place.

LIFE IS SWEET CHOCOLATE

STICKY TOFFEE TRUFFLES

★ **Makes 15–20 sticky nuggets**

★ **Take 20 minutes to make; set overnight.**

225g (8oz) dairy toffees
100g (4oz) pecan nuts
100g (4oz) dates
75ml (3fl oz) double cream
400g (14oz) milk chocolate, broken into small bits
25ml (1fl oz) instant espresso coffee
1 tsp groundnut oil

Sticky Toffee Pudding began life at the Sharrow Bay Hotel on the banks of Lake Ullswater, in Cumbria, where I once took my parents for afternoon tea. There was an unfortunate incident in the dining room involving golden syrup, children and kisses, all of which are prone to stickiness.

★ Place the dairy toffees in a plastic bag, sealing it well, then place the bag inside a tea towel and whack it with a rolling pin. Whack! That's for snoring all night. Whack! That's for ogling Miss Pettigrew in the butcher's. Whack! That's for deleting the computer website histories. In no time your toffees will be cudgelled into small crumbs with just a few desirable lumpy bits.

★ Choose 20 nice-looking pecan nuts and set them aside. Put the remaining pecans and all the dates into a food processor and whizz until they are all coarsely chopped.

★ Pop the cream into a saucepan and heat until very warm, without letting it boil. Be careful it does not burn or catch on the bottom of the pan. Remove from the heat.

★ Put half of the chocolate into a bowl and pour over the hot cream. Give it a brisk stir, add the espresso and set aside, but check to make sure that the chocolate has melted.

★ Add the chopped dates and pecans and the bashed toffees to the chocolate mixture and stir. Set aside in the fridge, preferably overnight, to firm up.

★ Line a flat 39 × 35cm (15¼ × 13¾in) baking sheet with a piece of baking parchment. Using a teaspoon, take a dollop of the chocolate mixture and, using the palms of your hands, roll it into a ball. Place the balls on the baking sheet. Be quick, as you don't want to melt the chocolate. Dispatch the tray of truffles to the fridge for about 30 minutes to firm up again.

★ Place 5cm (2in) of hot water in a pan and heat. Pop a heatproof bowl on top of the pan, making sure that the bottom of the bowl is not touching the water. Place the remaining chocolate and the groundnut oil into the bowl and gently warm until melted. Remove from the heat.

★ Carefully take each truffle ball and, using two forks, dip it into the melted milk chocolate until coated all over, letting any excess chocolate drip back into the bowl. Place the coated ball back on the baking sheet and pop one of the reserved whole pecan nuts on the top. Continue until all the balls are coated with the chocolate. Leave the coated balls to cool and set in a cool place.

MORNING COFFEE CUPS

Ladies, are you tired of ironing his shirts and scrubbing his smalls? Throw down your iron, banish the mop and call the gals over for a little chocolate cup laced with espresso – or six. Natter endlessly about jam covers, pie crusts, the stock market and quantum physics.

★ Place 5cm (2in) of water in a pan and heat. Pop a heatproof bowl on top of the pan, making sure that the bottom of the bowl is not touching the water. Place the dark chocolate and the butter in the bowl and gently warm until melted. Remove from the heat.
★ Add the espresso powder and stir well.
★ Pour the coffee-flavoured chocolate into a heatproof jug and divide the mixture between 25 small, foil sweet cases.
★ Place a chocolate-covered coffee bean on the top of each cup. Place the cups on a plate and leave to set in the fridge overnight.

★ **Makes 25 coffee cups**

★ **Take 15 minutes to make; cool and set overnight.**

400g (14oz) good-quality dark chocolate, broken into small bits
50g (2oz) butter
2 heaped tsp instant espresso powder
25 chocolate-covered coffee beans, to decorate

25 foil sweet cases

Handy Hint
After you have served your husband's dinner, whip him into a frenzy with your chocolate coffee cup shimmy.

CHILLI AND LIME SHARDS

★ **Makes about 10 spicy shards**

★ **Take 20 minutes to make; cool and set overnight.**

400g (14oz) good-quality dark chocolate, broken into small bits
25g (1oz) butter
Finely grated zest of 2 limes
2 tsp chilli flakes, to taste
½ tsp sea salt

Handy Hint
Place a scoop of good chocolate ice cream between two shards for a spicy twist on a classic choc-ice.

Miss Rosey Apple, the head sweet-taster at H and G, is taking her hubby on holiday to Mexico. When I told her that Montezuma drank 50 cups of chilli hot chocolate a day, in order to raise the chutzpah to service each of his 50 wives, she looked up from her spreadsheet, got all giddy and wistful, and flushed like a May Queen in a sausage shop.

★ Place 5cm (2in) of hot water in a pan and heat. Pop a heatproof bowl on top of the pan, making sure that the bottom of the bowl is not touching the water. Place the dark chocolate in the bowl and gently warm it to melt. Add the butter and stir until melted. Remove from the heat.
★ Once the mixture has cooled slightly, add the lime zest, half the chilli flakes and the sea salt. Stir until they are evenly distributed.
★ Pour the spicy chocolate onto a 39 x 35cm (15¼ x 13¾in) baking sheet lined with baking parchment and scatter the remaining chilli flakes over the top. Leave in a cool place to set – overnight is best. Once set, break lengthways into uneven shards and serve.

HOPE AND GREENWOOD

Fudge and Toffee

CHAPTER TWO

SPLENDID CONFECTIONERY

PULLED BUTTER TOFFEE

★ **Makes 20 good twists**

★ **Takes 30 minutes to make; a couple of hours to cool.**

Groundnut oil, for greasing
450g (1lb) granulated sugar
150ml (5fl oz) water
100g (4oz) butter
½ tsp cream of tartar

You will also need a pair of rubber gloves oiled with groundnut oil. (Yes, this is going to be fun all the way!)

This recipe is ideal if you are bothered by bingo arms, have a blacksmith as a neighbour or throw the shot putt as a hobby. You will need the strength of an ox, sir, and rubber gloves to make this very traditional butter toffee. It is enormous fun to make – with dramatic huffing and puffing, pulling and twisting. Next year I may bring out the accompanying fitness DVD.

★ Lightly oil a 39 x 35cm (15¼ x 13¾in) baking sheet with groundnut oil.
★ Put the sugar, water, butter and cream of tartar into a heavy-bottomed pan. Heat the mixture on a moderate heat, stirring all the time until the sugar has dissolved. Then bring the mixture to the boil and bubble until your sugar thermometer reaches 137°C (280°F).
★ Quick as sticks, pour the mixture onto the prepared baking sheet in an oozy puddle. Be careful, it is hotter than Tracy 'show me your hose', the fireman's daughter.
★ Once it is cool enough to handle (after about 20 minutes), don your best rubber gloves and oil them up with groundnut oil.

P.T.O.

★ Take two diagonally opposite corners of the puddle and pull them over into the middle of the toffee. Then take the other two opposite corners and pull them into the middle to almost meet the others. Now pull, pull and pull. Take two corners and stretch the toffee out like a long sausage, then take the ends and fold them into the middle. Take hold of the two 'new' ends and pull them out like a sausage again, fold them into the centre and keep repeating. Keep doing this until your Marigolds are exhausted (about 10 or 15 times). The toffee will turn into spaghetti-type strands. Now twist the strands together like a corkscrew to form tight barley twist ringlets. Chop into 5cm (2in) long sticks using some sturdy scissors.

★ Wrap in individual parchment twist wraps or pretty cellophane. The toffee will last longer than your granny so long as it is wrapped and kept dry.

Handy Hint
A rubber glove will give you the power you need to twist off any stubborn screwtop lid, they are also an intrinsic part of playing matron.

ENGLISH ALMOND BUTTER TOFFEE

Almond Butter Toffee is, without question, the George Clooney of toffees. If I was the last woman on earth and I had to choose between Clooney and his packet of English Almond Butter Toffee (and the existence of mankind depended on it), I'd definitely nibble his packet.

★ **Makes 25 lumps of almond heaven**

★ **Takes 30 minutes to make; about 6 hours in total to cool and set.**

Groundnut oil, for greasing
400g (1lb) flaked almonds
450g (15oz) butter
500g (1lb 2oz) granulated sugar
1 tsp vanilla extract
200g (7oz) milk chocolate, broken into small pieces

★ Preheat the oven to 95°C/200°F/Gas ¼. Grease a baking tin 42 x 27cm (16½ x 10¾in) and 4cm (1½in) deep with groundnut oil.
★ Place the almonds on a second, clean baking sheet and roast in the oven for 5–10 minutes, turning them over and around after 5 minutes and taking care not to singe the edges. Remove from the oven once golden and set aside to cool.
★ Place the butter in a deep, heavy-bottomed pan and melt it gently. Add the sugar and stir until it has dissolved. Place a sugar thermometer in the pan, bring the mixture to the boil and bubble on a medium heat until the thermometer reaches 120°C (250°F). This takes 5 minutes.
★ Add three-quarters of the toasted almonds and the vanilla extract to the sugar and butter mixture and give it a couple of brisk stirs with a wooden spoon. The mixture will bubble up a fair bit, so I have warned you. This takes about 5 minutes.

P.T.O.

★ Bring the mixture back to a rolling boil and, on a moderate heat, bubble slowly and steadily for around 15 minutes until the thermometer reaches 150°C (310°F). Take care, it will stay forever at 135°C (275°F) and then whoosh up to 148°C (300°F) before you can say 'acrid smoke-filled kitchen'. (This will take about 5 minutes.)

★ As soon as the temperature nudges 150°C (310°F), whip the pan off the heat and pour the golden mixture into the greased baking tin. Don't worry if it looks a little oily. Leave to cool for 1 hour.

★ Place the small pieces of chocolate evenly over the top of the still-warm toffee and leave to melt. Spread out the chocolate with a flat knife.

★ Grind the remaining almonds in a coffee grinder until roughly crumbed and scatter the crumbs over the melted chocolate, pressing down to make them stick. Leave to cool.

★ To remove the toffee from the tin, take a flat screwdriver or toffee hammer and stick it into the toffee and give it a good bash. Break it into chunks and store in the fridge.

Handy Hint

For some reason this toffee tastes best when served directly from the fridge.

CINDER TOFFEE

★ **Makes 20 or so lumps**

★ **Takes 30 minutes to make; 2 hours to cool and set.**

Groundnut oil, for
    greasing
450g (1lb) granulated
    sugar
300ml (½ pint) water
4 tbsp light malt vinegar
3 tbsp honey
1 tbsp liquid glucose
1 tsp bicarbonate of soda

You may know this toffee as a Crunchie Bar or Violet Crumble; as a Geordie I call it Cinder Toffee, as it looks like golden lumps of coal. However, if you are Australian you will most likely call it Honeycomb, if you are Irish it is Yellow Man. My Scottish chums call it Puff Candy, while inhabitants of NYC call it Sponge Candy. My tanned Californian friends call it Sea Foam, and if you hail from Wisconsin it is the delightful Fairy Food Candy.

Whatever you call it, this toffee above all toffees is by far the most dramatic to make; it volcanically bubbles to the top of your pan while being heated. I have controversially used honey in my recipe, which gives the toffee a wonderful flavour. Like it or lump it.

★ Grease a 23cm (9in) square baking tin (4cm/1½in deep) with groundnut oil.

★ Place the sugar, water, vinegar, honey and liquid glucose into a deep, heavy-bottomed pan. (When I say deep, I mean deep!) Heat on a moderate heat, stirring all the time, until the sugar has dissolved. Then bring the mixture to the boil.

★ Place a sugar thermometer in the pan and, without stirring, bubble the mixture until the thermometer reads 140°C (285°F) – this takes about 20 minutes.

P.T.O.

★ Combine the bicarbonate of soda with 2 teaspoons of cold water, mixing it well. Take the pan off the heat once it reaches the correct temperature, pour the soda into the toffee and give it a brisk stir. It will bubble up like a foaming sea right to the top of the pan; you will squeal with excitement and probably wish you had used a bigger pan. Don't say I didn't warn you …

★ Immediately pour the toffee into the prepared tin and leave to cool. When cold, prise the toffee out of the tin using a flat knife and break it up into chunks. If it is difficult to release from the tin, whack it with a hammer; I usually find this works for practically everything in life.

Handy Hint

To make Hokey Pokey, add crumbles of Cinder Toffee to vanilla ice cream.

PEANUT BUTTER FUDGE

I love peanut butter; I can't get enough of it. It is exceptional in a bacon sandwich or as a face mask, and it is beyond my wildest nut fantasies when added to this creamy fudge. I am informed that my American chums eat 3 pounds of peanut butter per person every year; apparently that's enough to cover the floor of the Grand Canyon. Now that would make your wellies sticky.

★ Line a 20cm (8in) square baking tin, 4cm (1½in) deep, with baking parchment.

★ Place the sugar, evaporated milk, double cream and butter into a deep, heavy-bottomed pan over a gentle heat. Stir the mixture with a wooden spoon until the sugar has dissolved – this takes about 5 minutes.

★ Turn up the heat to medium, place your sugar thermometer in the pan and bring the mixture to the boil – it will double in size, so put the cat in a safe place.

★ Bring the mixture up to 100°C (215°F), stirring occasionally, then lower the heat to a gentle boil. Boil for a further 10 minutes, but take care when the thermometer reaches 115°C (240°F), as at this point the mixture burns easily. Remove from the heat.

★ Using an electric hand whisk or food processor, or indeed a wooden spoon, beat the mixture for 10 minutes and then add the peanut butter. Beat for a further 15 minutes or until the mixture loses its shine, thickens up and starts to appear grainy. Pour into the prepared tin.

★ Set aside to cool. After about 1 hour, score the surface into rough squares with a knife. Once cold and firm, break into squares.

★ **Makes about 25–30 squares of salty joy**

★ **Takes 30 minutes to make; a couple of hours to set.**

500g (1lb 2oz) caster sugar
340ml (12fl oz) evaporated milk
2 tbsp double cream
100g (4oz) butter
2 large rounded tbsp crunchy peanut butter

Handy Hint
Please pop the finished fudge into a parcel and post it to: Miss Hope, 42 Peanut House, Peanut Head, Peanutsville.

CREAMY HONEY AND GINGER FUDGE

This delicious soft fudge is jewelled with nuggets of stem ginger and fecund with runny honey. Bears all over the world go wild for this; when you are safely tucked up in bed they raid your kitchen cupboards and poke their snouts in your fridge. More than once I have risen to discover a sated bear snoozing in my living room.

★ Line a 20cm (8in) square baking tin, 4cm (1½in) deep, with baking parchment.

★ Place the sugar, honey, butter, evaporated milk and cream into a deep, heavy-bottomed pan and gently heat until the sugar has dissolved, stirring with a wooden spoon. This takes 3–5 minutes.

★ Now turn up the heat to medium and place your sugar thermometer in the pan. Bring the mixture to a boil, stirring occasionally just to make sure the mixture does not stick to the bottom of the pan. Pay attention! After 15 minutes the mixture should have reached 100°C (212°F), now turn down the heat to a simmer, as it is at this point that the fudge is most likely to burn.

★ Keep heating until the mixture has reached 115°C (240°F), take the pan off the heat and, using an electric whisk, beat the mixture for 10 minutes. Add the chopped ginger and the syrup. Beat for a further 10 minutes until the fudge loses its gloss and goes grainy around the edges.

★ Pour into the prepared tin. After an hour or so, score the fudge with a knife to create squares. Once set, cut the fudge into rough squares.

★ **Makes about 25–30 squares**

★ **Takes 40 minutes to make; a couple of hours to cool (if you can wait that long).**

450g (1lb) granulated sugar
150ml (5fl oz) honey
75g (3oz) unsalted butter
200ml (7fl oz) evaporated milk
200ml (7fl oz) double cream
5 knobs of stem ginger (from a jar), chopped into small pieces, plus 2 tbsp of the syrup

Handy Hint
If you suspect there is a bear in your living room, please put your dressing gown on before going to investigate – bears are easily offended.

CREAMY CARAMELS

★ **Makes 30 or so chewy twist-tied chunks**

★ **Take 30 minutes-ish to make; 5–6 hours to cool.**

Groundnut oil,
  for greasing
350g (12oz) granulated
  sugar
2 tbsp liquid glucose
150ml (¼ pint) milk
250g (9oz) butter
150ml (¼ pint) double
  cream
2 tsp vanilla extract

Do you remember Merry Maids, the chewy, creamy caramels wrapped in cellophane decorated with a milkmaid carrying milk churns? I believe the maid in question was called Olga, she lived in the mountains and eventually, after a false start with a local yodelling teacher, settled down with a goat herder called George. She liked to make toffee. Here is my version of her unbeatable creamy caramels. You may wish to yodel while cooking – it is good for the goats.

★ Grease a 20cm (8in) square baking tin, 4cm (1½in) deep, with groundnut oil.
★ Place the sugar, glucose, milk and 75g (3oz) of the butter in a heavy-bottomed pan. Heat on a moderate heat, stirring all the time, until the sugar has dissolved. Bring the mixture to the boil and add another 75g (3oz) of butter.
★ Place a sugar thermometer in the pan and, without stirring, bubble the mixture until the thermometer reaches 112°C (235°F); this takes about 20 minutes. Now you may yodel.
★ While you are waiting, place the cream in a separate pan and warm it gently. Add the remaining butter and the vanilla extract, and stir until the butter has melted. Carefully pour the cream mixture into the sugar mixture.

P.T.O.

★ Bring the sugar and cream mixture back up to 112°C (235°F). Then take the pan off the heat and immediately pour the caramel into the prepared tin. Leave to cool in a cool place.

★ Once partially set, score lines on the surface of the caramel to mark out squares. When it has set, cut the caramel into cubes (scissors are the best tool for this, I find) and wrap each cube in a little parchment paper, twisting the ends.

Handy Hint

These caramels are even better when left to mature for a few days. Obviously they are never going to hang around for that long – they are far too moreish – but it is my duty as a confectioner to inform you of this.

LIFE IS SWEET FUDGE AND TOFFEE

CHOCOLATE ORANGE CARAMELS

Nell Gwynn would be proud to sell these squishy creamy caramels; I bet she'd even get her oranges pinched.

★ Grease a 20cm (8in) square baking tin, 4cm (1½in) deep, with groundnut oil.

★ Place the butter in a deep heavy-bottomed pan and gently and slowly heat it until it melts. Add the sugar and the golden syrup and condensed milk and continue to heat over a moderate heat, stirring constantly with a wooden spoon, until the sugar has dissolved.

★ Put your trusty sugar thermometer in the pan, bring the mixture to the boil and bubble until the thermometer reaches 110°C (230°F) – this takes 10–15 minutes. It should be golden in colour, like a retriever. Add the broken chocolate and stir briefly.

★ Bubble again, this time bringing the mixture up to 123°C (255°F); this will take 5 minutes. The mixture should be a darkish caramel colour, like a spray tan. Take the pan off the heat and stir in the grated orange zest.

★ Pour the caramel into the greased tin and leave to cool for 1 hour, then mark out squares in the surface with a knife. Leave to cool overnight before cutting into squares. Wrap each square in a gay twist of parchment paper.

★ **Makes 25 caramel squares**

★ **Take 30 minutes to make; cool and set overnight.**

Groundnut oil, for greasing
40g (1½oz) butter
225g (8oz) granulated sugar
150ml (¼ pint) golden syrup
200g (7oz) condensed milk
50g (2oz) orange chocolate bar, broken into small pieces
Finely grated zest of 1 orange

Handy Hint
These caramels taste even better when left to mature for a few days. Age before beauty, and all that.

SALT LIQUORICE CARAMELS

Liquorice is part-sweet, part-medicine. It is good for everything: the heart, stomach, colds, ulcers and spots. Roman soldiers kept some in their toga pockets and Napoleon sucked it to cure his bad breath.

★ Grease a 20cm (8in) square baking tin, 4cm (1½in) deep, with groundnut oil.

★ Place the liquorice in a pan and cover with the water. Bring to the boil and simmer for 20 minutes until the gloop is reduced to around 2 tablespoons. Take the pan off the heat and leave the mixture to cool and infuse for another 20 minutes, then pour the mixture into a food blender and whizz until it becomes a thick paste with no lumpy bits.

★ Place the butter in a deep, heavy-bottomed pan and melt slowly. Add the sugar, condensed milk and the golden syrup. Heat over a moderate heat, stirring constantly with a wooden spoon to dissolve the sugar.

★ Put a sugar thermometer in the pan and bring the mixture to the boil. Bubble until the thermometer reaches 110°C (230°F). It will be golden in colour. Add the liquorice paste and stir well.

★ Bubble again, this time bringing the mixture up to 123°C (255°F); this will take 5 minutes. The mixture should be black: black as night, black as a black sheep from the valley. Take the pan off the heat.

★ Pour the caramel into the prepared tin and scatter with rock salt. Leave to cool for 1 hour then mark out squares in the surface with a knife. Leave to cool overnight before cutting into squares. Wrap each square in a gay twist of parchment paper.

★ Makes 20–25 caramels

★ Take 30 minutes-ish to make; cool and set overnight.

Groundnut oil, for greasing
225g (8oz) soft black liquorice, cut into REALLY, REALLY small pieces
300ml (½ pint) water
75g (3oz) butter
450g (1lb) granulated sugar
400g (14oz) condensed milk
300ml (½ pint) golden syrup
1 good pinch of rock salt

Handy Hint
If you are lucky enough to have a stash of salt liquorice, substitute it with my blessing.

CRUMBLY VANILLA POD FUDGE

★ **Makes about 25–30 squares**

★ **Takes 30 minutes to make; a couple of hours to cool.**

700g (1lb 7oz) granulated sugar
75g (3oz) unsalted butter
200ml (7fl oz) evaporated milk
200ml (7fl oz) double cream
Seeds scraped from 1 vanilla pod

Jane Johnson – how I envied her! At 10 years old Jane was pure evil in a panama; when I was still wearing Start-rite T-bar shoes in the playground she was flaunting a lion cut and platforms. Once, her mother made this superb vanilla fudge for assembly; it was a secret recipe and far too special to share with the likes of me.

Now I have loads of fudge, it is far better than her mother's, and Jane is not getting any of it. So, ner-ner ner-ner-ner!

★ Line a 20cm (8in) square baking tin, 4cm (1½in) deep, with baking parchment.
★ Place the sugar, butter, evaporated milk and cream into a deep, heavy-bottomed pan and gently heat until all the sugar has dissolved, stirring with a wooden spoon. This takes 3–5 minutes. (You can check the sugar has dissolved by running a metal spoon through the mixture and looking on the back of the spoon for sugar crystals.)
★ Now turn up the heat to medium and place your sugar thermometer in the pan. Bring the mixture to a boil, stirring occasionally just to make sure the mixture does not stick to the bottom of the pan. After 15 minutes the mixture should have reached 100°C (212°F), now turn down the heat to a simmer, as it is at this point that the fudge is most likely to burn.

★ Keep heating until the mixture has reached 115°C (240°F). Take the pan off the heat. Using an electric whisk or food mixer, beat the mixture for 10 minutes. Add the vanilla seeds and beat for a further 10 minutes until the fudge loses its gloss and goes quite grainy around the edges.

★ Pour into the prepared tin. After an hour or so, score the fudge with a knife to create squares. Once set, snap the fudge into rough squares – and don't give any to Jane Johnson.

Handy Hint

Put the discarded vanilla pod into a jar of caster sugar and leave for a week or so. Voilà! Vanilla sugar used by angels, princesses, and organised cooks everywhere.

RUM AND RAISIN FUDGE

★ **Makes about
25–30 squares**

★ **Takes 30 minutes to
make; approx. 4 hours
for soaking and cooling.**

200g (7oz) raisins
4 tbsp dark rum
450g (1lb) dark
   muscovado sugar
450g (15oz) granulated
   sugar
250ml (8fl oz) double
   cream
2 tbsp golden syrup

Arr, me hearties, at Hope and Greenwood me beauties celebrate International Talk Like a Pirate Day come September. For all ye fudge pirates out there, this be a grog and raisin fudge, a-haaar, crammed with rum-soaked raisins and dark, Caribbean treacly sugars. A-haaar – it be shiverin' yer timbers and bracin' yer mainsail.

★ Line a 20cm (8in) square baking tin, 4cm (1½in) deep, with baking parchment.
★ Place the raisins in a bowl, keeping a small handful in reserve for decoration later. Cover with rum and leave the raisins for a couple of hours, or longer, to become quite sozzled.
★ Place the sugars, cream and golden syrup in a pan and stir until dissolved. Place your sugar thermometer in the pan and bring the mixture to the boil, bubbling until the thermometer reaches 115°C (240°F); this takes 10–15 minutes.
★ Take the pan off the heat and add the rum and raisins.
★ Using an electric whisk, food mixer or wooden spoon, beat the mixture for 10–15 minutes until the fudge loses its gloss and goes quite grainy around the edges.
★ Pour into the prepared tin and scatter over the reserved raisins.
★ After an hour or so, score the fudge with a knife to create squares. Once set, snap the fudge into rough squares.

Why are pirates called pirates?

Because they aaaar!

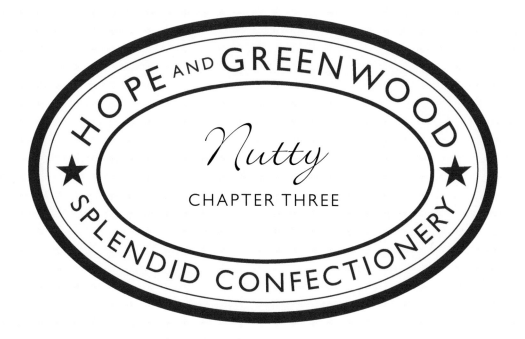

HOPE AND GREENWOOD

SPLENDID CONFECTIONERY

Nutty

CHAPTER THREE

MR GREENWOOD'S BUTTERED BRAZILS

★ **Makes 20–25 buttered nuts**

★ **Take 30 minutes to make; 1 hour to cool and set.**

200g (7oz) brazil nuts
225g (8oz) light brown
    sugar
75g (3oz) butter
½ tsp cream of tartar
50 ml (2fl oz) water
Groundnut oil, for
    greasing

Handy Hint
If your wife is not warm, throw a rug over her.

Mr Greenwood has long believed that the secret to happiness is a glass of Islay Malt Whisky, a documentary about rough seas, a roaring fire, a dish of Buttered Brazils and a warm wife. He is not far wrong.

★ Preheat the oven to 180°C/350°F/Gas 4.
★ Scatter the brazil nuts over a baking sheet and pop them in the oven for 10 minutes until slightly roasted and golden. Set aside to cool.
★ Place the sugar, butter, cream of tartar and water in a deep, heavy-bottomed pan and set over a low heat, stirring until the sugar has dissolved. (You can check the sugar has dissolved by running a metal spoon through the mixture and looking on the back of the spoon for sugar crystals.)
★ Put the sugar thermometer in the pan and bring the mixture up to the boil, without stirring. Carefully let it bubble until the thermometer reaches 132°C (270°F).
★ Lightly oil a 39 x 35cm (15¼ x 13¾in) baking sheet. Remove the pan from the heat and, using two forks, dip each brazil nut slowly and carefully into the hot toffee, briefly returning the toffee to the heat if it starts to dry.
★ Place the toffee-coated brazils on a clean baking sheet. Drizzle over any toffee left in the pan. Leave for an hour to cool and set.
★ Keep them in a cool, dry cupboard and they will last for a good five days or so.

LIFE IS SWEET NUTTY

SQUIRREL NIBBLES

One day Squirrel Greenwood said to himself, 'I will hop, I will skip, to the Great Oak Wood where I will play with the wood sprites and gather nuts and ting.' Before long it was really dark and a bit spooky, Squirrel Greenwood was cold and tired and really missed his mummy. Luckily, he had left a trail of acorns which, by the light of Lady Moon, he was able to follow all the way back to his yard. His mother was absolutely livid and grounded him for a week.

★ Preheat the oven to 200°C/400°F/Gas 6. Line a 39 × 35cm (15¼ × 13¾in) baking sheet with baking parchment.
★ Spread the nuts out over another baking sheet and place in the oven for 5–10 minutes until the nuts are toasty and golden. Remove from the oven and leave to cool.
★ Place 5cm (2in) of hot water in a pan and heat. Pop a heatproof bowl on top of the pan, making sure that the bottom of the bowl is not touching the water. Place the dark chocolate in the bowl with the groundnut oil and salt and gently warm it to melt. Remove from the heat.
★ Once the choccy has melted, stir in the roasted nuts.
★ Using a teaspoon or two, take a dollop of the nutty chocolate mixture and place it on the prepared baking sheet. Try to keep the nut piles tall rather than flat. (Squirrels are notoriously fussy.)
★ Set aside to cool and set for a couple of hours. When you can no longer bear the anticipation, eat them with aplomb.

★ **Makes 25–30 nutty nibbles**

★ **Take 20 minutes to make; about 3 hours in total to cool and set.**

200g (7oz) hazelnuts
100g (4oz) flaked almonds
200g (7oz) good-quality dark chocolate, broken into small pieces
1 tsp groundnut oil
A small pinch of salt

Handy Hint
You can add a handful of chopped dried figs to the chocolate for a little extra chewiness.

PECAN PIE CHUNKS

★ **Makes about 20 chocolatey chunks**

★ **Take 30 minutes to make; cool and set overnight.**

200g (7oz) pecans
400g (14oz) plain
  chocolate
200ml (7fl oz) double
  cream
2 tbsp golden syrup
2 tbsp bourbon

If Mr Greenwood had his way, every day would be pie day; it would be an all-day running pie buffet: wall-to-wall pie, pie city. Now that I've merged pecan pie with a chocolate bar, full of luscious golden syrup and bourbon, all Mr G's dreams have come true.

★ Preheat the oven to 200°C/400°F/Gas 6. Line a 20cm (8in) square baking tin (4cm/1½in deep) with baking parchment.
★ Pop the pecans onto a clean baking sheet and place in the oven for 5–10 minutes until roasty and toasty. Set aside to cool, then roughly chop them.
★ Break the chocolate into small pieces and place in a bowl.
★ Heat the cream, syrup and bourbon in a pan. When the mixture is reasonably warm to hot, pour it over the chocolate and stir until all the chocolate has melted.
★ Mix the pecans into the chocolate mixture then pour the chocolate gunge into the prepared tin and leave to set – overnight is best.
★ Once set, break into uneven chunks and eat with a strong coffee and an elasticated waistband.

Handy Hint
It is very important to stick your finger in the mixture at least five times, just to make sure you like it.

LIFE IS SWEET NUTTY

SPICED CASHEW CHUNKS

When Mr. Greenwood had hair he also had a chum called Pete.
Pete had a nut-loving pet monkey called Fearless Freddie.
In 1973 they opened a shop on the Old Kent Road selling spiced
cashews with the entrepreneurial addition of a chocolate
coating. Freddie is now a millionaire and lives in Torremolinos.

★ Preheat the oven to 200°C/400°F/Gas 6. Place the cashews on
a 39 x 35cm (15¼ x 13¾in) baking sheet.
★ Place the honey, butter, cayenne and cinnamon in a small pan, stir
and heat gently until runny. Pour the honey mixture over the cashews,
stir them up and place them in the oven for about 10 minutes – the
honey should be bubbling and the cashews beautifully golden. Remove
from the oven and leave to cool completely.
★ Place 5cm (2in) of hot water in a pan and heat. Pop a heatproof
bowl on top of the pan, making sure that the bottom of the bowl is
not touching the water. Place the dark chocolate into the bowl and
gently warm it to melt. Remove from the heat.
★ Line a 20cm (8in) square baking tin, 4cm (1½in) deep, with baking
parchment. Reserve a dozen or so whole cashews nuts for decorating
– I know you want to eat them, but do as you are told. Now place a
piece of baking parchment over the top of the remaining cashews,
grab your rolling pin and roll and bash away at the nuts – use all that
pent-up supermarket-trolley rage – until they are coarsely battered.
★ Mix the cashews with the melted chocolate and pour into your lined
baking tin. Scatter over the remaining cashews and leave to cool and
set overnight. Once set, cut the cashew chocolate into rough chunks.

★ **Makes 15–20 chunks**

★ **Take about 30 minutes
to make; cool and set
overnight.**

200g (7oz) salted
    cashew nuts
3 tbsp honey
25g (1oz) butter
½ tsp cayenne pepper
¼ tsp ground cinnamon
400g (14oz) good-quality
    dark chocolate, broken
    into small bits

PEANUT PRETZEL KNOBBLIES

★ **Makes 20 knobbly nibbles**

★ **Take 15 minutes to make; set overnight.**

200g (7oz) milk chocolate, broken into small pieces
100g (4oz) crunchy peanut butter
175g (6oz) salted pretzels, roughly broken up
A good pinch of rock salt

These lip-smacking knobblies are made from broken pretzels, peanut butter and milk chocolate. The ref blows his whistle; the crowds roar; you kick off; it's Salt City V Sugar Town in your Tastebud Stadium; he's dribbling all the way…It's a GOAL!

★ Line a 39 x 35cm (15¼ x 13¾in) baking sheet with baking parchment.
★ Place 5cm (2in) of hot water in a pan and heat. Pop a heatproof bowl on top of the pan, making sure that the bottom of the bowl is not touching the water. Place the milk chocolate in the bowl and gently warm to melt.
★ Remove the pan from the heat and add the peanut butter, stir really well, then add the broken pretzels.
★ Using a teaspoon, place small clusters of pretzel chocolate on the baking sheet. Try to keep the knobblies tall rather than wide, like a Wembley flagpole. Scatter with rock salt. Leave to set for a few hours, though overnight is better.

Handy Hint

Peanut Pretzel Knobblies are excellent with a cold beer and flipflops.

LIFE IS SWEET NUTTY

VICTORY
CHOCOLATE
BARS

CONTROLLED
PRICE
3d. each
PRODUCT GROUP
C1

NELSON, LANCS.

MARZIPAN SANDWICHES

★ **Makes 25–30 colourful sandwiches**

★ **Take 45 minutes to make, plus 1 hour to cool.**

400g (14oz) ground almonds
50g (2oz) icing sugar
450g (1lb) granulated sugar
150ml (¼ pint) water
½ tsp cream of tartar
½ tsp almond extract
Green food colouring
Pink food colouring
50g (2oz) good-quality dark chocolate, broken into small bits
30 almond slivers, to decorate

Well, hey nonny nonny and off with your head, here we are in merrie 17th-century England dining on that culinary delight, the 'marchpane'. It took an Elizabethan servant about 100 years to grind the almonds and sugar required to make this doublet-tightening cake, and many were fatally suffocated – falling exhausted, ruff first, into the sticky mixture.

As luck would have it, you probably have a food mixer, so death by marchpane-suffocation proves no threat.

★ Stir the ground almonds and icing sugar together and pop into a food mixer.

★ Place the granulated sugar and water into a heavy-bottomed pan and place it on a low heat. Stir continuously with a wooden spoon until the sugar has dissolved. This may take 5–10 minutes, so please be patient.

★ Put a sugar thermometer in the pan, bring the mixture to a boil and add the cream of tartar. Bubble gently for around 10–15 minutes until the syrup reaches 115°C (240°F) on the thermometer.

★ Turn on the food mixer and gently add the syrup to the ground almonds in a steady shining thread. Add the almond extract and mix well. Leave to cool for 10 minutes then remove the paste from your food mixer and set aside until it is cool enough to handle.

P.T.O.

LIFE IS SWEET NUTTY

★ Divide the mixture into three equal lumps:

★ To lump 1 add a few drops of green food colouring and then knead the paste until it is the pale green of a leprechaun's waistcoat.

★ To lump 2 add pink food colouring and knead well until it is the colour of a princess's petticoat.

★ For lump 3, place 5cm (2in) of hot water in a pan and heat. Pop a heatproof bowl on top of the pan, making sure that the bottom of the bowl is not touching the water. Place the dark chocolate in the bowl and gently warm to melt. Then add the melted chocolate to the paste and knead until it is the brown of a squirrel's hankie.

★ Place each lump between two pieces of cling film and then, using a rolling pin, roll them out until they are roughly rectangular and approximately ½cm (⅛in) thick and about 13 x 22cm (5 x 9in).

★ Then layer one rectangle of paste on top of another to make a sandwich. I favour a green layer, then brown, then pink, but the choice is yours. Run the rolling pin lightly over the marzipan sandwich to squidge the pastes together.

★ Cut the marzipan into small, even squares and decorate each with a sliver of almond.

Sugar Gossip

Queen Elizabeth snacked on sugary stuff so much that her teeth were black. The crazy ladies in her court followed suit, blackening their teeth and painting their faces white to ape their beloved queen.

LIFE IS SWEET NUTTY

ORANGE WALNUT CANOODLES

Once you have succumbed to my creamy orange chocolate and chewy walnut praline canoodles you may find yourself seeking out other orange pleasures. Space Hoppers, goldfish, jolly big carrots, hamsters, plastic cheese, traffic cones and polyester flares are all orange, but not nearly as tempting as a canoodle.

★ Preheat the oven to 200°C/400°F/Gas 6. Lightly oil a 39 × 35cm (15¼ × 13¾in) baking sheet.

★ Place the walnuts on the baking sheet and shove them in the oven for 5–10 minutes until they are roasted. Take them out and put them aside to cool. Reserve 25 walnuts for decoration and whizz the rest in a coffee grinder.

★ Place the sugar and 2 tablespoons of water into a small, heavy-bottomed pan and stir over a low heat until the sugar has dissolved. Bring to the boil and bubble for 1–2 minutes.

★ Stir the ground walnuts into the sugar syrup. Once cooled and hand-hot, return the mix to the coffee grinder and give them a second whizz.

★ Place 5cm (2in) of hot water in a pan and heat. Pop a heatproof bowl on top of the pan, making sure that the bottom of the bowl is not touching the water. Place the dark chocolate in the bowl and gently warm it to melt. Remove from the heat.

★ Add the orange zest then the walnut crumbs to the chocolate. Stir well then pour the mixture into the sweet cases lined up on a baking sheet. Decorate the top of each canoodle with a reserved walnut.

★ Makes 20–25 cups

★ Take 30 minutes to make; cool and set overnight.

Groundnut oil, for greasing
100g (4oz) walnuts
50g (2oz) granulated sugar
200g (7oz) dark chocolate, broken into small bits
Finely grated zest of 1 large orange

20–25 sweet cases

Handy Hint
Try swapping the walnuts for almonds or macadamias, if you must meddle.

PROPER PEANUT BRITTLE

★ **Makes 20 nutty shards**

★ **Takes 45 minutes to make; a couple of hours to cool.**

Groundnut oil, for greasing
350g (12oz) shelled unsalted peanuts
400g (14oz) granulated sugar
100g (4oz) soft brown sugar
150ml (5fl oz) golden syrup
100g (4oz) butter
150ml (5fl oz) water
¼ level tsp bicarbonate of soda

Handy Hint
This is hot, really hot. Don't even think about putting the toffee pan directly onto your kitchen worksurface, it will burn it. I know this from experience.

If you have a spare moment perhaps you could ape (yes, that was a monkey-nut pun) my American chum Mr Tom Miller, who pushed a peanut to the top of Pike's Peak (14,100 feet) using his nose in 4 days, 23 hours, 47 minutes and 3 seconds. Alternatively, you could enjoy peanuts by staying home, making some proper crunchy peanut brittle and watching the telly.

★ Preheat the oven to 180°C/350°F/Gas 4. Lightly oil a 20 x 30cm (8 x 12in) toffee tin 2.5cm (1in) deep (see Stockists on page 126).
★ Scatter the peanuts onto another baking sheet and place them in the oven for 10 minutes until golden, take care not to let them burn.
★ Pop both sugars, the golden syrup, butter and water into a deep, heavy-bottomed pan and heat gently until the sugar has dissolved.
★ Put a sugar thermometer in the pan and bring the mixture to the boil. Boil very gently for at least 30 minutes, probably more, until your sugar thermometer reaches 149°C (300°F). It will seem like forever, but don't be tempted to turn up the heat as the toffee will burn very easily. Be patient – pat your hamster while you wait.
★ Chuck in the bicarbonate of soda and roasted peanuts and chuckle with glee as the mixture bubbles up to the top of the pan like Vesuvius. Remove from the heat.
★ Carefully pour the toffee into the prepared tin and leave to cool. Once cool attack the toffee with your toffee hammer, breaking it into lumps. If you have not invested in a toffee tin you will have to stick a screw driver into it to break it up – this involves a bit of swearing.

FRUIT AND NUT SQUARES

★ **Makes 30 nibbles**

★ **Take about 45 minutes to make; cool and set overnight.**

100g (4oz) shelled whole
   hazelnuts
40g (1½oz) raisins
175g (6oz) caster sugar
1 egg white
A pinch of sea salt
Icing sugar, for dusting
150g (5oz) good-quality
   dark chocolate, broken
   into pieces
1 tsp groundnut oil

This almost-healthy little chocolate is for all you hunter-gatherers out there with strong muscles and hairy chests. The succulent raisins and hazelnuts are easily plucked during a morning stroll through long grasses with your handwoven reed trug, while the chocolate is easily gathered from your corner shop on your way to the launderette.

Please note that this recipe contains raw egg white which isn't good for old people, pregnant ladies or children. If you stand to inherit large sums, cook this for your mother and stand well back.

★ Preheat the oven to 95°C/200°F/Gas ¼. Line a 39 x 35cm (15¼ x 13¾in) baking sheet with baking parchment.
★ Place the hazelnuts on another baking sheet and stick them in the oven for 5–10 minutes until they are golden and roasted. Leave to cool for 30 minutes or so.
★ Reserve 15 hazelnuts for decoration and put the rest in a coffee grinder. Whizz the nuts until they are a pleasing crumb size.
★ Reserve 30 whole raisins for later then finely chop the remainder.
★ Place the sugar, nuts and raisins in a bowl and add the egg white and salt. Get stuck in and, using your hands, squidge the mixture until it is a firm paste. And stop whinging, you've had your hands in worse.

LIFE IS SWEET NUTTY

★ Throw a wodge of icing sugar onto your very clean, no cat paw prints, worksurface and roll out the paste until it is 5mm (¼ in) thick. Cut into equal-sized squares. Gather up the straggly bits and repeat the process until all the paste is cut.

★ Place 5cm (2in) of hot water in a pan and heat. Pop a heatproof bowl on top of the pan, making sure that the bottom of the bowl is not touching the water. Place the dark chocolate and the groundnut oil into the bowl and gently warm it to melt. Remove from the heat and allow it to cool for 5 minutes.

★ Now, using two spoons, dip the squares into the melted chocolate, letting the excess chocolate drip back into the bowl. Slide each square onto the lined baking sheet. Finely chop the reserved hazelnuts and, while the chocolate is still wet, place a reserved raisin on top of each square and sprinkle the hazelnuts over.

Handy Hint

If you are a real-life hunter-gatherer, well done – keep up the foraging.

COCONUT ICE

There are a million grillion ways to make coconut ice, but here
is mine. It is soft, yielding and ultimately chewy. Better still,
you don't have to cook it at all, but you do need the muscles
of Martin the Muscleman and his Banana of Steel.

I firmly believe coconut ice should be pink, really pink. This
is not a moment to get all modern idealist with me, young lady.
What harm can a drop of pink really do? Remember when you
were six years old and you ate worms and put peanuts up your
nose, nothing bad ever happened, did it?

★ Line a 20cm (8in) square baking tin (4cm/1½in deep) with cling film.
★ Sift the icing sugar into a bowl, then add the condensed milk and,
starting with a wooden spoon, stir the mixture. Then roll up your
sleeves, get stuck in with your hands and knead the mixture.
★ Gradually add the coconut, kneading the stiffening mixture until
all the coconut is mixed in. It's hard work and takes a little while, but
just think of someone you don't like that much – your boss perhaps,
or your ex. I like to think of Mr Greenwood and his cartoon snoring.
★ Split the mixture in half. Press the first half into the lined baking tin,
pressing it down with heel of your hand.
★ Colour the remaining half pink using the food colouring – it can
be as pink as you wish. Mix it well.
★ Take small balls of the pink mix and place them over the white
coconut mix in the tin. With your hand, press the pink mixture over
the white to form an even layer.
★ Allow to set for a few hours – overnight is best. Cut into squares.

★ Makes 15–20 rinky-
dink pink squares

★ Takes 30 minutes to
make, set overnight.

500g (1lb 2oz) icing sugar
2 x 397g cans condensed
milk
400g (14oz) desiccated
coconut
Pink food colouring

Handy Hint

*Eating worms or
putting peanuts up your
nose would be rather
foolish, especially
at your age.*

HOPE AND GREENWOOD

*Mallows
and Nougat*

CHAPTER FOUR

SPLENDID CONFECTIONERY

MALLOWS D'AMOUR

★ **Makes around 25 tokens of squishy love**

★ **Take 45 minutes to make; 2 or more hours to set.**

Icing sugar and
   cornflour, to dust
450g (1lb) granulated
   sugar
1 tbsp liquid glucose
1 sachet of powdered
   gelatine
3 tbsp rose syrup
5–6 drops of pink food
   colouring
2 large egg whites
Crystallised rose petals,
   to decorate

Shame on you, this is not a reference to your special attributes but to beautiful pink, heart-shaped, squishy mallows infused with the delicate scent of roses. Scatter them around your boudoir, on your bed, or in the bath.

★ Line a 20cm (8in) square baking tin (4cm/1½in deep) with baking parchment and, using a sieve, shake equal amounts of icing sugar and cornflour over the base until the parchment is lightly dusted.

★ Put the sugar, glucose and 200ml (7fl oz) of water into a heavy-bottomed pan and give it a quick stir. Place your sugar thermometer in the pan, bring the liquid to a gentle boil and continue cooking for about 25–30 long minutes until the mixture reaches 127°C (260°F) on the thermometer.

★ While you are waiting, sprinkle the gelatine over 100ml (4fl oz) of boiled water (following the instructions on the packet), making sure it has dissolved properly. Add the rose syrup and the pink food colouring to the dissolved gelatine.

★ When the syrup reaches the correct temperature, remove the pan from the heat and remove the sugar thermometer. Pour the dissolved gelatine into the syrup. Be careful, it will bubble and spit and rise to the top of the pan.

P.T.O.

★ Drag your food mixer (plus whisk attachment) or electric whisk out from the back of the cupboard and whisk the egg whites together until stiff. Still whisking, slowly add the syrup and gelatine mixture to the eggs. With the mixer or whisk on a super-fast setting, whisk for a further 25–30 minutes until the mixture is thick, shiny and holding its shape reasonably well on the whisk. You can snog a bit while you are waiting.

★ Spoon the mallow mixture into the dusted tin and leave it to set for about two hours. Dust a second piece of parchment with equal amounts of icing sugar and cornflour. Turn the mallow out onto the paper. Dust a heart-shaped cutter with cornflour and icing sugar and cut the mallow into heart shapes. Dust the cut edges and leave to dry on a wire rack.

★ Place the mallows into a receptacle of your choice and scatter with crystallised rose petals.

Handy Hint

Miss Mallows d'Amour can be seen performing her famous fan dance the length and breadth of Great Britain.

LIFE IS SWEET MALLOWS AND NOUGAT

RASPBERRY MARSHMALLOWS

I had the enormous pleasure of making this truly delicious, fresh raspberry-studded, sticky, fluffy, marshmallow for my friends at the Rosey O'Conner's Hip and Thigh exercise class. The ladies there were so excited they fashioned me a throne out of Ryvita crackers and crowned me with a Vanilla and Chocolate Müller Light with sprinkles.

★ Line a 20cm (8in) square baking tin (4cm/1½in deep) with baking parchment and, using a sieve, shake equal amounts of icing sugar and cornflour over the base until the parchment is lightly dusted.
★ First, make the raspberry coulis. Place roughly half the fresh raspberries in a pan with the caster sugar (set the other half aside for decoration later). Cook on a medium heat for around 10 minutes, stirring until it is a lovely ruby-red mush. Strain the mixture into a clean bowl, pressing the pulp through a sieve with the back of a metal spoon. Leave to cool.
★ Put the sugar, glucose and 200ml (7fl oz) of water into a heavy-bottomed pan and give it a quick stir. Place your sugar thermometer in the pan, bring the liquid to a gentle boil and continue cooking for about 15 long minutes until the mixture reaches 127°C (260°F) on the thermometer.
★ While you are waiting, sprinkle the gelatine over the 100ml (4fl oz) of hot water (following the instructions on the packet), and check to make sure it has dissolved properly.

★ **Makes around 25 cubes**

★ **Take about 1 hour to make; 2 hours to set, plus 2–3 hours to cool.**

Icing sugar and cornflour, to dust
450g (1lb) granulated sugar
1 tbsp liquid glucose
1 sachet of powdered gelatine
2 large egg whites

For the raspberry coulis
300g (11oz) fresh raspberries
2 tbsp caster sugar

P.T.O.

★ When the syrup reaches the correct temperature, remove the pan from the heat and remove the thermometer. Pour the dissolved gelatine into the syrup. Be careful – it will bubble and spit a little and rise to the top of the pan – it is extremely hot.

★ Locate your food mixer (plus whisk attachment) or electric whisk and whisk the 2 egg whites together in a large mixing bowl until stiff. Still whisking, slowly add the syrup and gelatine mixture to the eggs. With the mixer or whisk on a fast setting, whisk for a further 20–25 minutes until the mixture is thick, shiny and holding its shape reasonably well on the whisk.

★ Using a spoon, gently fold the raspberry coulis through the mallow mixture to create a rippled effect. Spoon half the mallow mixture into the dusted tin and place half the reserved raspberries over the top. Spoon the remainder of the mallow mix over the top of the fresh raspberries, smoothing the top with a flat knife if necessary, then scatter the remaining raspberries over the top.

★ Leave the mallow to set for about 2 hours. Dust a second piece of parchment with icing sugar and cornflour. Turn the mallow out onto the paper. Cut into squares, dust the cut edges and leave to dry on a wire rack.

Handy Hint

Make a white chocolate dipping sauce to go with this. Melt 200g (7oz) of white chocolate in a heatproof bowl over a pan of simmering water, pour into a clean bowl and dip away.

LIFE IS SWEET MALLOWS AND NOUGAT

CANDIED PEEL AND WHITE CHOCOLATE NOUGAT

★ **Makes 25–30 squares**

★ **Takes 30 minutes to make; cool and set overnight.**

100g (4oz) white chocolate, broken into little bits
2 large egg whites
400g (14oz) caster sugar
125ml (4½fl oz) runny honey
210ml (7½fl oz) liquid glucose
A pinch of salt
Seeds scraped from 1 vanilla pod
200g (7oz) candied peel (lemon, orange or grapefruit), roughly chopped

You will also need 3 sheets of rice paper (sometimes called edible wafer, it can be found in the baking section of your supermarket)

If you are short of time and don't want to make your own candied peel (even though it is the best candied peel in the world and can be found on pages 116–119) you will find suppliers of good candied peel on page 126. If you live in big London, jump on a red bus and get yourself off to Fortnum & Mason, who have a surfeit of delicious peels.

★ Line a 20cm (8in) square baking tin (4cm/1½in deep) with the rice paper.
★ If you are making your own candied peel, do this first – simply follow my recipe but do not add the chocolate coating.
★ Put the white chocolate bits into a freezer bag and put it in the freezer, where it will play hospitals with the fish fingers.
★ Place the egg whites in a food mixer and whisk until stiff.
★ Place the sugar, honey and liquid glucose into a deep heavy-bottomed pan and add 2 tablespoons of water. Heat gently until the sugar has dissolved.
★ Place a sugar thermometer in the pan, bring the honey mixture to the boil and bubble until the temperature reaches 125°C (260°F), the mixture should be a buttery, golden colour. This takes 10–15 minutes. With the food mixer running, take the pan off the heat and pour half the honey mixture into the egg white in a thin ribbon, slowly does it. Leave the mixer running until I tell you to stop.

★ Quickly return the pan to the heat, increase the heat slightly and bring the honey mixture up to 157°C (315°F) on your sugar thermometer, this will take 10 minutes. The mixture should be a dark, caramel colour. Pour the remaining honey mixture into the food mixer, slowly. Add the salt and the vanilla seeds then mix on a moderate speed for a full 10 minutes.

★ Now you can turn the mixer off.

★ Next, take the chocolate out of the freezer and fold it and the candied peel into the nougat – it will be fairly stiff.

★ Pour the nougat into the prepared tin and leave it to set, preferably overnight. Cut into small squares when firm.

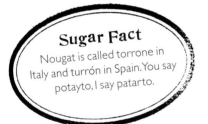

Sugar Fact

Nougat is called torrone in Italy and turrón in Spain. You say potayto, I say patarto.

Handy Hint

If this recipe does not set it is because you have
a) Ignored the temperatures like a crazy person, or
b) Not beaten it for long enough. Please do not come crying to me because it has gone floppy.

CHERRY AND
ALMOND NOUGAT

Sticky but firm, oozy and sweet, I'd like to make this nougat my best friend; we could cuddle up at the pictures together and maybe stop for a shandy in the town. I love you Cherry and Almond Nougat, I really do.

★ Preheat the oven to 200°C/400°F/Gas 6. Line a 20cm (8in) square baking tin (4cm/1½in deep) with the rice paper.
★ Place the almonds onto a clean baking sheet and pop in the oven to roast for 5–10 minutes. Set aside to cool.
★ Place the egg whites in a food mixer and whisk until stiff.
★ Place the sugar, honey and glucose into a deep, heavy-bottomed pan. Add 2 tablespoons of water. Heat gently to dissolve the sugar. Put a sugar thermometer in the pan, bring the honey mixture to the boil and bubble until your thermometer reaches 125°C (260°F). With the food mixer running, take the pan off the heat and slowly pour half the honey mixture into the egg whites in a thin ribbon. Leave the mixer running.
★ Quickly return the pan to the heat, increase the heat slightly, and bring the remaining honey mixture up to 157°C (315°F). The mixture should be a dark, caramel colour. Pour this honey mixture into the food mixer, slowly. It will froth up to the top of the mixing bowl. Mix on a moderate speed for a full 10 minutes. Now you can turn the mixer off.
★ Fold in the almonds, cherries and vanilla seeds; the nougat will be reasonably stiff now. Pour the nougat into the prepared baking tin and leave to set, preferably overnight. Cut into small squares.

★ **Makes 20 sticky lumps**

★ **Takes 30 minutes to make; cool and set overnight.**

200g (7oz) whole almonds
2 large egg whites
400g (14oz) caster sugar
100ml (4fl oz) runny honey
210ml (7½fl oz) liquid
    glucose
200g (7oz) glacé cherries
Seeds scraped from
    1 vanilla pod

You will also need 3 sheets of rice paper

ORANGE HOT CHOCOLATE WITH MALLOW WANDS

★ **Makes enough for 2 admirably**

★ **Take 20 minutes to make, if using shop-bought mallows.**

For the hot chocolate
570ml (1 pint) milk
Peeled zest of 1 orange
2 tsp granulated sugar
100g (4oz) good-quality dark chocolate, broken into small pieces

For the wands
½ tsp ground cinnamon
1 tbsp icing sugar
6 cubes of marshmallow (see pages 94–95) or a packet of pink and white marshmallows

You will also need 2 wooden skewers

One dark wintry day, when the scudding clouds were scattering an icing-sugar frosting of snow over the gasworks, I decided to make this heavenly marriage of hot chocolate, orange, mallows and cinnamon as a 4 o'clock treat for the ladies at Sugar HQ. As luck would have it, 12 out of 10 of them loved it.

★ Pour the milk into a saucepan with the orange zest and slowly bring it to a simmer. Take off the heat and allow the orange zest to infuse into the milk for around 15 minutes.

★ Next, make the wands. Mix the ground cinnamon with the icing sugar and coat the marshmallow cubes in the sugary dust. Slot 3 mallow cubes onto the end of each skewer and set them aside.

★ Remove the orange zest from the milk. Place the milk back on the heat; add the sugar, stirring until all the sugar has melted.

★ Place the broken chocolate in a heatproof jug, pour the hot milk over the chocolate and stir until melted. Pour into mugs and serve with the mallow wands on the side for dipping and dunking, swirling and scooping.

FLUFFY VANILLA MARSHMALLOWS

★ **Makes around 15 pillows of cuddly mallows**

★ **Take 45 minutes to make; 2–3 hours to set.**

Icing sugar and
   cornflour, to dust
450g (1lb) granulated
   sugar
1 tbsp liquid glucose
1 sachet of powdered
   gelatine
2 large egg whites
Seeds from 1 vanilla pod

If Mr Greenwood were an honourable type of fellow he would marry a marshmallow, fluffy and warm as they are. They would have an egg-white wedding; they would cuddle all day long, safely cocooned under a duvet of icing sugar; he would father a brood of mini mallows who he would teach to swim in warm bowls of hot chocolate.

★ Line a 20cm (8in) square baking tin (4cm/1½in deep) with baking parchment and, using a sieve, shake equal amounts of icing sugar and cornflour over the base until the parchment is lightly dusted.

★ Put the sugar, liquid glucose and 200ml (7fl oz) of water into a heavy-bottomed pan and give it a quick stir. Place your sugar thermometer in the pan, bring the liquid to a gentle boil and continue cooking for about 15 long minutes until the mixture reaches 127°C (260°F) on the thermometer.

★ While you are waiting, sprinkle the gelatine over 100ml (4fl oz) of hot water (following the instructions on the packet), and check to make sure it has dissolved properly.

★ When the syrup reaches the correct temperature, remove the pan from the heat and remove the thermometer. Pour the dissolved gelatine into the syrup. Be careful – it will bubble and spit a little and rise to the top of the pan – it is extremely hot, the swine.

★ Drag your food mixer (plus whisk attachment) or electric whisk out from the back of the cupboard and, in a clean bowl, whisk the 2 egg whites together until stiff (see Handy Hint, below). Still whisking, slowly add the syrup and gelatine mixture to the egg whites. Add the vanilla seeds and then, with the mixer or whisk on a fast speed, whisk for a further 15–20 minutes until the mixture is thick, shiny and holding its shape on the whisk. If you are like me you will lean your elbow on the Kenwood and just watch it going round and round. It's tragic really.

★ Spoon the mallow mixture into the tin and leave to set for about 2 hours. Dust a second piece of baking parchment with equal amounts of icing sugar and cornflour. Turn the mallow out onto the paper. Cut into squares, dust the cut edges and leave to dry on a wire rack.

Handy Hint

To guarantee stiff egg whites, run the cut side of a lemon around the surface of the mixing bowl to remove any fat.

SHERBET LEMON MARSHMALLOWS

★ **Makes around 25–30 tingle-tastic cubes**

★ **Take about 1 hour to make; up to 2 hours to set.**

Icing sugar and
 cornflour, to dust
450g (1lb) granulated
 sugar
1 tbsp liquid glucose
200ml (7fl oz) water
1 sachet of powdered
 gelatine
Finely grated zest and
 juice of 2 lemons
2 large egg whites
2 tsp yellow food colouring
100g (4oz) lemon sherbet
 crystals, to decorate

I was partaking of lady lemonade one day when I had the glorious idea of combining the tingly lemon fizz with the sugary sweetness of marshmallow. A big hit with the ladies at Sugar HQ, I am duty-bound to share this tingly, lemon-sherbet-dipped mallow recipe with all my lemon-squeezing chums.

★ Line a 20cm (8in) square baking tin (4cm/1½in deep) with baking parchment and, using a sieve, shake icing sugar over the base until the parchment is lightly dusted.

★ Put the sugar, liquid glucose and 200ml (7fl oz) of water into a large, heavy-bottomed pan and give it a quick stir. Place your sugar thermometer in the pan, bring the liquid to a gentle boil and continue cooking for about 20–30 long minutes until the mixture reaches 127°C (260°F) on the thermometer.

★ While you are waiting, sprinkle the gelatine over 100ml (4fl oz) of hot water (following the packet instructions), making sure it has dissolved properly. Stir in the lemon zest and juice. Set aside.

★ When the syrup reaches the correct temperature, remove the pan from the heat and remove the thermometer. Pour the dissolved gelatine into the syrup. Be careful, it will bubble and spit and rise to the top of the pan – it is extremely hot.

P.T.O.

★ Using an electric mixer or whisk, whisk the 2 egg whites together until stiff. Still whisking, slowly add the syrup and gelatine mixture to the eggs. Add the yellow food colouring. Then, with the mixer on super fast, whisk for a further 20–25 minutes until the mixture is thick, shiny and holding its shape reasonably well on the whisk.

★ Spoon the mallow mixture into the dusted tin and leave it to set for about 2 hours. Dust a second piece of parchment with equal amounts of icing sugar and cornflour. Turn the mallow out onto the paper. Cut into squares using a knife dipped in hot boiled water; press the cut edges into the lemon sherbet crystals and leave to dry on a wire rack.

Handy Hint
If you pop the lemon into the freezer for 10 minutes first, it makes it much easier to grate.

LIFE IS SWEET MALLOWS AND NOUGAT

VERY BAD S'MORES

First recorded in the *Girl Scout Handbook* of 1927, S'mores (give me 'some more') are an American campfire treat, the delights of which have been tragically overlooked in Blighty. In my 'no-bonfire-required' version, gooey mallows, runny chocolate and digestive biscuits are all squished together in a shocking oozy dribbly mess. (Have plenty of wet wipes and perhaps a spare clean T-shirt to hand!)

★ **Makes 4 S'mores**

★ **Take 5 minutes to make.**

100g (4oz) bar of dark or milk chocolate, broken into squares
8 digestive biscuits
8 pink and white marshmallows
Dulce de Leche toffee sauce

★ Preheat the grill. On a baking sheet, place 1 square of chocolate onto 4 of the digestive biscuits. Top each with 2 mallows and drizzle over a dollop of toffee sauce.
★ Place the biscuits under a grill until brown and bubbling. Remove from the heat.
★ Squidge the remaining 4 digestive biscuits on top.

VARIATIONS
★ Swap the toffee sauce for peanut butter.
★ Add chocolate ice cream after you have grilled the mallows.
★ Use pieces of orange chocolate instead of milk chocolate.
★ Use ginger snap biscuits instead of digestive biscuits.

UNICORN MALLOWPOPS

★ **Makes 6 fairytale lollies**

★ **Take 20 minutes to make; a couple of hours to set.**

100g (4oz) sweet microwaveable popcorn
50g (2oz) unsalted butter
200g (7oz) pink and white marshmallows
Groundnut oil, for greasing
6 wooden lolly sticks

I once kept a unicorn as a pet; she was called Jenny. I brushed her golden mane every day with a Mason Pearson hairbrush and polished her horn with Pledge Classic Beauty until it shone. They were the happiest days of my life. One day I came home to find Mr G. had sold her to the circus, where she now performs the dangerous triple somersault with Tony Curtis.

★ Following the packet instructions, place the popcorn in the microwave and pop it. Open the bag and pour it into a bowl. Eat a handful. (Oh, come on, don't pretend you don't want to, no one is looking and I won't tell.)

★ Put the butter into a pan and melt it gently. Add the mallows and cook on a low heat for 10 minutes, stirring from time to time, until the mallows have melted.

★ Pour the mallow mess over the popcorn and stir it around and around, like a record, baby. Leave the mallow and popcorn muddle to cool for about 30 minutes.

★ Take a lump of the mixture, a little larger than a golf ball, and squeeze the mixture into a cone or horn shape between your hands. Really give it a good squeeze so that all the popcorn sticks together firmly. This is enjoyably squidgy and sticky – well, I enjoy it anyway. Place on a lightly oiled 39 × 35cm (15¼ × 13¾in) baking sheet to set.

★ Leave to set for a couple of hours, then push a lolly stick into the wide base of each cone and munch away.

HOPE AND GREENWOOD

Fruity

CHAPTER FIVE

SPLENDID CONFECTIONERY

ROSE AND PISTACHIO TURKISH DELIGHT

★ **Makes 30 rosy jellies**

★ **Takes 1½ hours to make; chill and set overnight.**

Groundnut oil, for greasing
900g (2lb) granulated sugar
1 tbsp lemon juice
175g (6oz) cornflour
1 tsp cream of tartar
2 tbsp rose syrup
2–3 drops pink food colouring
100g (4oz) shelled pistachios
Icing sugar and cornflour, to dust

Turkish delight was originally eaten as a cure for sore throats. Known as *'lokum rahat'*, it literally translates as 'throat's ease'. This sweetly scented rose and pistachio Turkish delight is as soft and bouncy as Miss Penelope 'Jugs' Jones, the juggler's daughter. It takes an age to make, but it is really worth the effort.

★ Line a 20cm (8in) square baking tin (4cm/1½in deep) on all sides with baking parchment and lightly oil it with groundnut oil.

★ Place the sugar, lemon juice and 340ml (12fl oz) of water in a pan and put it over a low heat. Stir until all the sugar has dissolved. Bring the mixture to the boil, without stirring, and slowly, using your sugar thermometer, bring the mixture up to 118°C (245°F) – this will take about 15 minutes.

★ Meanwhile, in a separate pan (this one must be really deep and truly heavy bottomed), place the cornflour, 570ml (1 pint) cold water and the cream of tartar. Give it a good stir and place over a low heat. Keep stirring so that there are no lumps (it's like making cheese sauce). Bring to the boil and beat quickly until the mixture looks like wallpaper paste. Take it off the heat. This is strangely satisfying.

P.T.O.

★ Place the cornflour mixture back on the heat; as soon as the sugar mixture has reached 118°C (245°F) pour it over the cornflour mixture. Stir it well – it will look like an ocean of icebergs – and if any lumps persist, whisk them out with a metal whisk. Keeping the heat low, bring the mixture to a geyser-plopping simmer. Let it simmer like this, plopping and sighing, for an hour – yes, an hour.

★ Take the pan off the heat, stir in the rose syrup, the pink food colouring (as much or as little as you like) and the pistachio nuts. Pour the pink blubber into the prepared tin and leave to cool and set overnight. It smells amazing.

★ Once set, cut the Turkish delight into squares and dust with equal amounts of icing sugar and cornflour sifted together.

Sugar Trivia

Turkish delight can be found in Charles Dickens's *The Mystery of Edwin Drood* as 'lumps of delight', it is also the confection to which Edmund succumbs in *The Lion, The Witch and The Wardrobe*, and it features in Madonna's song 'Candy Shop'.

LIFE IS SWEET FRUITY

TROPICAL TRUFFLES

When one considers the fact that falling coconuts kill 150 people every year, it is amazing that folk go out at all. Luckily, you can make my Tropical Truffles in the safety of your home.

★ Place 5cm (2in) of water in a pan and heat. Pop a heatproof bowl on top of the pan, making sure the bottom of the bowl is not touching the water. Place the double cream, coconut cream, lime zest and juice in the bowl. Once hot, add the white chocolate, stir until melted. Set aside in the fridge to cool and thicken, preferably overnight.

★ Preheat the oven to 200°C/400°F/Gas 6. Drive a nail into one of the dimples at the top of the coconut. Discard the milk. Pop the coconut into a carrier bag and place on the ground and whack it with your trusty housewife's hammer. Pick the white flesh out of the coconut shell with a knife, then grate the flesh, leaving the brown skin behind. Place the grated coconut onto a baking sheet and toast in the oven for 5 minutes. Remove from the oven and leave to cool.

★ Line a flat 39 x 35cm (15¼ x 13¾) baking sheet with a piece of parchment paper. Using a teaspoon take a dollop of the truffle mixture and, roll it into a ball. Be quick as you don't want to melt the chocolate.

★ Place 5cm (2in) of water in a pan and heat. Pop a heatproof bowl on top of the pan, as before, and place the dark chocolate and groundnut oil in the bowl. Gently warm the chocolate until melted.

★ Carefully take each truffle ball and, using two forks, dip the ball in the melted dark chocolate until coated all over. Place the truffle on the baking sheet. Sprinkle over some toasted coconut while the chocolate is still wet. Continue until all the balls are coated with the chocolate.

FRUITY LIFE IS SWEET

★ **Makes 15–20 zingy zesty truffles**

★ **Take 20 minutes to make and about 2 hours in total to cool and set overnight.**

150ml (5fl oz) double cream
50g (2oz) coconut cream (in a block)
Finely grated zest and juice of 1 lime
200g (7oz) white chocolate, broken into small bits

For the dark chocolate coating
100g (3oz) good-quality dark chocolate, broken into small bits
1 tsp groundnut oil
Flesh of ½ a fresh coconut

Handy Hint
Always keep your housewife's hammer in a handy place. Nothing stops your husband blabbering about his tough day in the office like a hammer in one hand and your fourth G'n'T in the other.

RHUBARB AND CUSTARD CRUMBLE CUPS

★ **Makes 25 cups**

★ **Take 30 minutes to make; cool and set overnight.**

For the crumble
25g (1oz) plain flour
25g (1oz) butter, cut
   into small cubes
25g (1oz) demerara sugar

For the chocolate
100g (4oz) good-quality
   rhubarb and custard
   boiled sweets
400g (14oz) white
   chocolate, broken
   into small pieces
Seeds scraped from
   1 vanilla pod
1 drop of pink food
   colouring

25 foil sweet cases

Hope and Greenwood's rhubarb and custard is the finest in the land. It is in the pantries of celebrities and royalty. It deserves a knighthood and cloak of glory, free bus rides and complementary bread for the ducks in St James's Park.

★ Preheat the oven to 180°C/350°F/Gas 4.
★ For the crumble, sift the flour into a bowl, add the butter and then, using your fingers, rub the mixture until it resembles breadcrumbs. Add the demerara sugar and give it a good stir. Spread the mixture over a 39 x 35cm (15¼ x 13¾in) baking sheet and pop into the oven for 10 minutes until the crumble is golden brown. Take it out of the oven and set it aside to cool.
★ Leave the rhubarb and custard sweets in their wrappers and whack them with a rolling pin to break them up a bit. Remove the wrappers and place the bashed sweets in a coffee grinder and give them a whizz.
★ Place 5cm (2in) of water in a pan and heat. Pop a heatproof bowl on top of the pan, making sure that the bottom of the bowl is not touching the water. Place the white chocolate in the bowl and gently warm it to melt. Remove from the heat.
★ Add the vanilla seeds and a drop of pink food colouring. Stir in the rhubarb and custard sweet 'grounds' and mix well.
★ Pour the pink chocolate into a heatproof jug and divide it between the foil sweet cases. Sprinkle a little of the crumble mixture on top of each chocolate cup. Leave them to set, preferably overnight.

TWINKLY BLACKCURRANT FLOWERS

Children across the land will love to make this simple recipe. Cheer as fondant is squished into the shag pile and weep tears of joy as you Febreze icing sugar off the sofa. I have used Ribena, yes Ribena, I know it sounds odd but HP Sauce, Heinz Ketchup, Marmite, London Gin and Ribena are simple classics I would not be without. You also need a few children who like all things twinkly and pink.

★ Pour the double cream and Ribena into a bowl and mix it well.
★ Sieve the icing sugar over the cream mixture and stir to combine. Knead the mixture until it resembles bread dough – this only takes about 1 minute and the children will love getting stuck in. If the fondant seems a little runny, just add some more icing sugar until the dough resembles Play-Doh.
★ Wrap the fondant in cling film and pop in the fridge for 30 minutes to firm up.
★ Place a sheet of cling film on your worksurface and dust with icing sugar. Put the ball of fondant on top. Place another piece of cling film on top of the fondant. Using a rolling pin, roll out the fondant until it is about 1cm (½in) deep. Cut the fondant into flower shapes using a biscuit cutter and place them on a 39 x 35cm (15¼ x 13¾in) baking sheet. Press a silver ball into the centre of each flower and sprinkle with pink iridescent edible glitter. Set aside until firm.
★ The fondants will last about a week if stored in an airtight container.

★ **Makes about 20 twinkling flowers**

★ **Take 15 minutes to make; 1 hour to set.**

2 tbsp double cream
3 tbsp Ribena (undiluted)
275g (10oz) icing sugar, plus extra for rolling
Silver balls, to decorate
Pink iridescent edible glitter (I used Disco Baby Pink), to decorate

You will also need a small flower biscuit cutter (or a heart or butterfly would be pretty too)

Handy Hint
Go shopping and leave your mother in charge of cleaning up.

FRUITY LIFE IS SWEET

TOFFEE APPLES

★ **Makes 6**

★ **Take 30 minutes to make.**

6 small English
  knobbly apples
Butter, for greasing
6 liquorice root sticks,
  or 6 wooden lolly sticks
  (or indeed get out in
  the garden and acquire
  6 reasonably sturdy
  twigs – not poisonous
  ones – complete with
  the odd leaf or two)

For the toffee
200g (7oz) granulated
  sugar
100ml (4fl oz) cold water
1 tsp white wine vinegar
125ml (4½fl oz) golden
  syrup
25g (1oz) butter

I am a real stickler for traditional Hallowe'en fare, such as these sticky toffee apples with liquorice root 'stalks'. A walk in The Oak Wood is not complete without a warm pocket of buttery bonfire toffee, ginger beer and the odd soul cake. The word Hallowe'en is short for All Hallows' Eve, and if you spell Hallowe'en without the apostrophe I will get really quite cross with you.

★ Wash the apples and pop them into the fridge for a couple of hours, this will help the toffee stick to the apple.

★ Lightly grease a 39 x 35cm (15¼ x 13¾in) baking sheet with butter.

★ Put the sugar into a large, heavy-bottomed pan with 100ml (4fl oz) of cold water. Heat gently for 5 minutes until the sugar has dissolved. Stir with a wooden spoon occasionally and check for any remaining sugar crystals on the back of a metal spoon.

★ Add the vinegar, golden syrup and butter. Put a sugar thermometer in the pan and bring to a gentle boil on a medium heat. Bubble away until the thermometer reaches 127°C (260°F). This may take up to 30 minutes, but don't be tempted to whack the heat up or the toffee will burn in an instant, your smoke alarm will go off and you will have to flap about with a tea towel.

P.T.O.

LIFE IS SWEET FRUITY

★ While you are waiting for the caramel to reach the correct temperature, whittle the end of your sticks to a point. Push one stick into the stalk end of each apple; push it in hard as it needs to be firm and sturdy. I know you know how.

★ Remove the caramel from the heat. Pick up the first apple by its stick and dip it into the caramel to coat completely, turning it round and round, humming a little tune about elves and bonfires.

★ Place the apple, bum-side down, on the baking sheet and leave to cool. Repeat with the remaining apples.

VARIATIONS

S'MORE TOFFEE APPLES

Scatter a handful of miniature marshmallows and 3 crumbled chocolate digestives into the toffee just before you dip the apple.

NUTTY TOFFEE APPLES

Add a handful of chopped nuts to the toffee before dipping the apple into it.

LIFE IS SWEET FRUITY

MAPLE WALNUT PEARS

If you like toffee apples but are somewhat fickle, try these hopeylicious maple walnut pears. The pears are coated in a golden toffee, laced with sticky maple syrup and studded with walnuts. They are perfectly joyous in the leaf-rustly autumn months, especially with a crackling bonfire and a flagon of spiced cider.

★ Wash the pears and pop them in the fridge for a couple of hours; this will help the toffee stick to the pears.
★ Lightly grease a 39 × 35cm (15¼ × 13¾in) baking sheet with butter.
★ For the maple toffee, put the sugar into a large, heavy-bottomed pan with 100ml (4 fl oz) water. Warm it gently for 5 minutes until the sugar has dissolved, it should turn a lovely golden brown.
★ Add the vinegar, maple syrup and butter. Put a sugar thermometer in the pan and bring the mixture to a gentle boil on a medium heat. Boil until the mixture reaches 127°C (260°F). This may take up to 30 minutes, but don't be tempted to increase the heat or the toffee will burn.
★ While you wait, whittle the end of your sticks to a point. Push one stick into the stalk end of each of your pears; push it in hard, as it needs to be firm and sturdy.
★ Remove the caramel from the heat. Pick up the first pear by its stick and dip it into the caramel to coat completely, turning it round and round while humming a little tune about hedgehogs and wood goblins.
★ Place the pear, bum-side down, onto the baking sheet and scatter with chopped walnuts. Leave to cool. Repeat with the remaining pears.

★ **Makes 6 sticky pears**

★ **Take 30 minutes to make; a couple of hours to cool.**

6 small, ripe dessert pears
Butter, for greasing
6 liquorice root sticks
    (or 6 wooden lolly sticks)

For the maple toffee
200g (7oz) golden
    granulated sugar
1 tsp white wine vinegar
125ml (4½fl oz) maple
    syrup
25g (1oz) butter
100g (4oz) walnuts,
    finely chopped

CANDIED PEELS

★ **Makes 25 strips of sugared pleasure**

★ **Take about 50 minutes to make; about 4 hours in total to cool and set.**

2 oranges, unwaxed,
   organic
75g (3oz) granulated
   sugar
1 vanilla pod
175ml (6fl oz) water
Caster sugar, for dusting
100g (4oz) milk chocolate,
   broken into small pieces
1 tsp groundnut oil

Candied peel is everything good; it is sparkling with a frost of sugar crystals, full of citrus feel-good aromas and tastes jolly fine into the bargain. Oh, how green with envy will Brenda be when you pop round with a cake enriched with your very own home-made candied peel.

LET'S START WITH ORANGE PEEL
★ Peel the oranges carefully, leaving as much bitter white pith attached to the orange as you can. Cut the peel lengthways into strips about 5mm (¼ in) thick.
★ Put the peel into a small, deep pan and add enough cold water to just cover the peel. Bring the water to the boil, drain and refill with the same amount of cold water again. Bring to the boil and repeat twice (so three times in total). This takes about 30 minutes. Lean an elbow on your worktop and while away several minutes watching it boil.
★ After the final draining, add the sugar and vanilla to the pan of peel with 175ml (6fl oz) of water. Stir until the sugar has dissolved and then bring to the boil until the peel is soft and yielding, about 10 minutes. It smells fantastic. Remove the peel from the heat and leave to cool.
★ Drain off the syrup and dip each strip of peel into a bowl of caster sugar, coating it evenly all over. Place on a wire rack to become crisp and sugar crusted.
★ Place 5cm (2in) of hot water in a pan and heat. Pop a heatproof bowl on top of the pan, making sure that the bottom of the bowl

P.T.O.

LIFE IS SWEET FRUITY

is not touching the water. Place the milk chocolate and the groundnut oil in the bowl and gently warm to melt.

★ Scrape the sugar from one end of the peel. Dip the peel into the chocolate and place on a sheet of baking parchment to set.

NOW YOU CAN TRY LUSCIOUS LEMON PEEL

2 lemons, unwaxed, organic
100g (4oz) granulated sugar
125ml (4½fl oz) water
Caster sugar, for dusting
100g (4oz) good-quality dark chocolate, broken into small pieces
1 tsp groundnut oil

★ Peel the lemons carefully, leaving as much bitter white pith attached to the lemon as you can. Cut the peel lengthways into strips about 5mm (¼in) thick.

★ Put the peel into a small, deep saucepan; add enough cold water to just cover the peel. Bring the water to the boil, drain and refill with the same amount of cold water again. Bring to the boil and repeat twice (so three times in total). This takes about 30 minutes.

★ After the final draining, add the sugar to the pan of peel with the 125ml (4½fl oz) of water. Stir until the sugar has dissolved and then bring to the boil until the peel is soft and yielding, about 10 minutes. Remove the peel from the heat and leave to cool.

★ Drain off the syrup and dip each strip of peel into a bowl of caster sugar, coating it evenly all over. Place on a wire rack to become crisp and sugar crusted.

★ Place 5cm (2in) of hot water in a pan and heat. Pop a heatproof bowl on top of the pan, making sure that the bottom of the bowl is not touching the water. Place the dark chocolate and groundnut oil in the bowl and gently warm to melt.

★ Scrape the sugar from one end of the peel. Dip the peel into the chocolate and place on a sheet of baking parchment to set.

OR ZESTY GRAPEFRUIT

★ Peel the grapefruit carefully, leaving as much bitter white pith attached to the grapefruit as you can. Cut the peel lengthways into strips about 5mm (¼ in) thick.

★ Put the peel into a small, deep pan; add enough cold water to just cover the peel. Bring the water to the boil, drain and refill with the same amount of cold water again. Bring to the boil and repeat twice (so three times in total). This takes about 30 minutes.

★ After the final draining, add the sugar to the pan of peel with 175ml (6fl oz) of water. Stir until the sugar has dissolved and then bring to the boil until the peel is soft and yielding, about 10 minutes. Remove the peel from the heat and leave to cool.

★ Drain off the syrup and dip each strip of peel into a bowl of caster sugar, coating it evenly all over. Place on a wire rack to become crisp and sugar crusted.

★ Place 5cm (2in) of hot water in a pan and heat. Pop a heatproof bowl on top of the pan, making sure that the bottom of the bowl is not touching the water. Place the white chocolate in the bowl and gently warm it to melt.

★ Scrape the sugar from one end of the peel. Dip the peel into the chocolate and place on a sheet of baking parchment to set.

1 grapefruit,
    unwaxed, organic
75g (3oz) granulated
    sugar
175ml (6fl oz) water
Caster sugar, for dusting
100g (4oz) white
    chocolate, broken into
    small pieces

CHERRY CHAPEL HAT PEGS

★ **Makes 20 hat pegs**

★ **Take 30 minutes to make; 1 week to soak the cherries, plus cool and set overnight.**

1 jar of maraschino
    cherries
Kirsch (you will use
    about a ¼ bottle)
350g (12oz) good-quality
    dark chocolate, broken
    into small bits
200ml (7fl oz) double
    cream
25g (1oz) butter
1 tsp groundnut oil

20 sweet cases (optional)

So, you old romantic you, here are my amazing ganache-rich, kirsch-soaked cherry chapel hat pegs for your edification. Grown men are known to perk up after one nibble of these rich cherry chocolates, ladies swoon in the street, and granddad will reminisce about Betty Bright, his first love.

★ Get ahead: empty the liquid out of the cherry jar and fill it right up to the top with kirsch instead. Put the lid back on and leave it for a week to hibernate. After a week, drain the cherries, reserving the kirsch liquid.

★ Line a 39 x 35cm (15¼ x 13¾in) baking sheet with baking parchment.

★ Put 200g (7oz) of the broken chocolate into a bowl.

★ Pop the cream and butter into a saucepan and heat until simmering, without letting it boil. Be careful it does not burn or catch on the bottom of the pan.

★ Take the pan off the heat, pour it over the chocolate and give it a brisk stir. Set aside, but check it to make sure that all the chocolate has melted. Give it a stir to help it along if need be. Add 2 tablespoons of the reserved kirsch and stir.

★ Cool the mixture for an hour or so and then spoon dollops the size of a pound/euro/quarter coin onto the baking sheet. Once you have 20 dollops, go back and pop another dollop on top of the original dollop – try to keep the dollops quite tall.

P.T.O.

★ Place a cherry on top of each dollop, pressing it down slightly. Leave to set in a cool place.

★ Place 5cm (2in) of hot water in a pan and heat. Pop a heatproof bowl on top of the pan, making sure that the bottom of the bowl is not touching the water. Place the remaining dark chocolate and groundnut oil in the bowl and gently warm it to melt. Remove from the heat.

★ Carefully take each cherry dollop and, using two forks, dip it in the melted dark chocolate until coated all over. Place the coated dollop onto the baking parchment. Continue until all the dollops are coated with the chocolate. Leave the coated hat pegs to cool and set.

Handy Hint

If, like me, you like to titillate, take a pot of edible gold paste and a paint brush and gild the top of each hat peg with a simple flick of the wrist.

LIFE IS SWEET FRUITY

PEACH AND APRICOT PASTILLES

Mr Greenwood loves my wobbly jellies, and who can blame him? In Latin, apricot means 'precious', and indeed these sweet little jellies twinkle away like sugary jewels. Full of luscious apricots and peaches, the jellies are made with pectin rather than gelatine. Pectin can be found in the sugar aisle in your supermarket (I used Certo).

★ Line a 20cm (8in) square baking tin with baking parchment and grease it with butter.

★ Place the fruit in a saucepan and cover with 150ml (¼ pint) water. Put over a moderate heat and simmer. Simmer for 15 minutes until the fruit has softened.

★ Pop the fruit in a food processor and whizz until well puréed, with no lumps.

★ Place the purée and the sugar into a deep pan with 50ml (2fl oz) of water and the lemon juice and heat until the sugar has dissolved. Put a sugar thermometer in the pan, bring to the boil and bring the mixture very slowly up to 1185°C (245°F). This will take a good 30 minutes.

★ Add the butter and stir, cook for 2 more minutes.

★ Take the pan off the heat and pour in the pectin – it will bubble halfway up the pan (that's the fun bit), but give it a good stir.

★ Pour the jelly into the prepared tin and leave to cool and set overnight. Once set, cut into squares and coat with granulated sugar.

★ The pastilles will last for 2–3 days and should be kept in the fridge.

★ **Makes 30 firm jellies**

★ **Take 45 minutes to make; set overnight.**

1 tbsp butter, plus extra for greasing
125g (4½oz) no-soak dried peaches
200g (7oz) no-soak dried apricots
475g (17oz) granulated sugar, plus extra for coating
3 tbsp lemon juice
250ml (8fl oz) bottle of liquid apple pectin

Handy Hint
Once you have mastered peaches and apricots, experiment with other fruits such as strawberries or lemons.

PAVLOVA ISLANDS

My grandmother will tell you that she once toured with Anna Pavlova and was at dinner when the chef at the Wellington Hotel presented Anna with the very first fruit-filled meringue that came to be known as a 'Pavlova'. She will also tell you that the moon is a great big silver sixpence and that the people next door stole her telly.

★ Line a 20cm (8in) square baking tin (4cm/1½in deep) with cling film.

★ Place 5cm (2in) of hot water in a pan and heat. Pop a heatproof bowl on top of the pan, making sure that the bottom of the bowl is not touching the water. Place the white chocolate in the bowl and gently warm it to melt. Remove from the heat and leave to cool for 10 minutes.

★ Crumble the meringue nests roughly, setting aside a generous handful of crumble for the decoration.

★ Mix the cherries and berries into the melted chocolate then stir in the crumbled meringue. Dollop all the mixture into the lined baking tin so it fills the tin but is nice and lumpy. Top this with the reserved meringue pieces, pressing them down to make sure they stick to the surface of the chocolate.

★ Set aside until cold (overnight is best) and then break into chunks.

★ **Makes about 25 white-chocolate meringue chunks**

★ **Take 20 minutes to make; cool and set overnight.**

100g (3½oz) meringue (about 4 nests)
800g (1lb 12oz) white chocolate, broken into small pieces
200g (7oz) dried cherries and berries

Handy Hint
If your neighbour has stolen your telly, put the radio on.

STOCKISTS

Here is a list of jolly stockists where you will find some of the more troublesome ingredients and items used in my recipes. As if by magic (a click of a button or a tinkle on the phone), wonderful goodies will be delivered to your kitchen.

Our Hope and Greenwood shops supply all manner of sweet delight, including lemon sherbet crystals, rhubarb and custard sweets, coffee beans, toffees and toffee slab, liquorice root, Bassett liquorice sticks, 100g 73 per cent dark chocolate bars, milk and white chocolate bars. You can visit one of our two London stores, or you can shop for your supplies from the comfort of your armchair.
www.hopeandgreenwood.co.uk

Baking sheets and tins, sugar thermometers, biscuit cutters, vanilla extract, almond extract, natural wooden lolly sticks and toffee trays complete with a toffee hammer.
www.lakeland.co.uk

Pink sprinkles, any sprinkles, edible gold leaf, peppermint oil, sugar thermometers, silver balls, sweet and petits fours cases.
www.jane-asher.co.uk

Liquid glucose and pectin.
www.tesco.com or www.sainsburys.co.uk

Heart-shaped cutters, flower cutters – any cutter you could ever dream of.
www.cakecraftshop.co.uk

Rose and violet syrups, crystallised rose and violet petals (oh, the beauty).
www.confiserieflorian.com

Bamboo skewers.
www.colanderscookshop.co.uk

Candied peel, baby figs, dates, dried apricots, dried figs, raisins, hazelnuts, almonds, pecans and stem ginger.
www.juliangraves.com

INDEX